MW01030067

Presented To:

_____

From:

_____

Date:

_____

# DEMON
# PROOFING
# PRAYERS

# DEMON
# PROOFING
# PRAYERS

## BOB LARSON'S GUIDE TO SPIRITUAL WARFARE

BOB LARSON

© Copyright 2011–Bob Larson

All rights reserved. This book is protected by the copyright laws of the United States of America. This book may not be copied or reprinted for commercial gain or profit. The use of short quotations or occasional page copying for personal or group study is permitted and encouraged. Permission will be granted upon request. Unless otherwise identified, Scripture quotations are taken from the New King James Version. Copyright © 1982 by Thomas Nelson, Inc. Used by permission. All rights reserved. Scripture quotations marked NASB are taken from the NEW AMERICAN STANDARD BIBLE®, Copyright © 1960, 1962, 1963, 1968, 1971, 1972, 1973, 1975, 1977, 1995 by The Lockman Foundation. Used by permission. Scripture quotations marked NIV are taken from the HOLY BIBLE, NEW INTERNATIONAL VERSION®, Copyright © 1973, 1978, 1984 International Bible Society. Used by permission of Zondervan. All rights reserved. Scripture quotations marked NLT are taken from the Holy Bible, New Living Translation, copyright 1996, 2004. Used by permission of Tyndale House Publishers., Wheaton, Illinois 60189. All rights reserved. Scripture quotations marked TLB are taken from The Living Bible; Tyndale House, 1997, © 1971 by Tyndale House Publishers, Inc. Used by permission. All rights reserved. All emphasis within Scripture quotations is the author's own. Please note that Destiny Image's publishing style capitalizes certain pronouns in Scripture that refer to the Father, Son, and Holy Spirit, and may differ from some publishers' styles. Take note that the name satan and related names are not capitalized. We choose not to acknowledge him, even to the point of violating grammatical rules.

DESTINY IMAGE® PUBLISHERS, INC.

P.O. Box 310, Shippensburg, PA 17257-0310

*"Promoting Inspired Lives"*

This book and all other Destiny Image, Revival Press, MercyPlace, Fresh Bread, Destiny Image Fiction, and Treasure House books are available at Christian bookstores and distributors worldwide.

For a U.S. bookstore nearest you, call **1-800-722-6774.**

For more information on foreign distributors, call **717-532-3040.**

Reach us on the Internet: **www.destinyimage.com.**

ISBN 13 TP: 978-0-7684-3930-4

ISBN 13 Ebook: 978-0-7684-8947-7

For Worldwide Distribution, Printed in the U.S.A.

2 3 4 5 6 7 8 9 10 11 / 13 12 11

# Foreword

Would you like to "demon-proof" your life?

Demon-Proofing Prayers is NOT about how to do deliverance, but rather how to avoid needing deliverance, how to be a spiritual warrior to keep you and those you love safe from the oppression of the enemy.

If anyone on earth knows how to proof against demons, it's my friend, Bob Larson! Bob Larson's ministry of deliverance spans more than three decades, with 15,000 documented case studies of exorcism. His efforts to set the captives free have taken him to 100+ countries, and he has seen the work of Satan in many cultures and religious contexts. Bob understands how the devil's kingdom operates, and he brings these practical insights to this book.

These very special prayers and confessions are designed to keep you in spiritual victory, protected against the assignments Satan has on your life. These confessions and acclamations will introduce you to a whole new way of living beyond the bondage of a demon-harassed life to the joy and liberty of a demon-proofed life.

Don't just read this book. Make its prayers a part of your daily life, an antidote for all the demonic attacks coming your way each day.

By Bobb Biehl, Executive Mentor

Visit www.BobbBiehl.com to get a detailed introduction to the many high visibility consulting clients Bobb has worked with in the areas of personal and organizational development. His web site gives you access to the hundreds of practical *"leadership, management, life tools"* he has developed, including 20 published books. Bobb has over 40 years of board experience and has consulted with over 200 boards. He has advised over 500 Presidents, Senior Pastors, and Directors and over 5,000 executive staff members, investing over 50,000 hours on a one to one basis.

"Strengthening Christian Leaders Internationally Since 1976."

# Contents

PART II ACTIVATIONS:
### Ten Prayerful Proclamations to Demon-Proof Your Life

Introduction

# Understanding Prayer as Warfare Against the Devil and His Demons

T HE first time I encountered a demon was in Singapore some 40 years ago. As a young single man and a comparatively new Christian, I had embarked on a long solo trip through many countries. I ended up in Singapore at just the right time to witness a Hindu ceremony called Thaipusam in honor of the god Shiva and the goddess Kali.

Demons are more overt in many places in Asia and India than they are in the United States, where they invade academia and the intelligentsia and hide behind "scientific inquiry" and "reason." When you talk to Asians and Indians about the spirit world, they know what you're talking about because demons make their presence known there on an almost daily basis.

The day swirled with sights, sounds, and strange rituals, including the self-mutilation of devotees. One of them took three-foot steel skewers and pushed them all the way through one cheek and out the other. Another one extended his tongue, took a sharp knife and pierced it vertically, and left the knife in so he could not retract his tongue. Others took hundreds of fish hooks and put them into their backs and chests—and then they would hang objects from the hooks in order to rip and tear at the flesh. Some took spike shoes with the nails pointed upward and strapped them onto their feet. Others flailed themselves with knives or inserted huge meat hooks into the muscles of their backs so they could tow an idol through the streets. Hundreds of people, mostly men, were doing this. In spite of all the torture, I never saw a single drop of blood.

I asked people, "Why don't you bleed?" The answer was always the same: "Our god does this to show his power." Though I was new to my faith, that idea seemed like the antithesis of the Gospel of Jesus. It was a bloodless gospel that was not really good news to anybody. These people were so far gone in a trancelike oblivion that they didn't even know what was happening to them. They would start at one temple and end up six or eight hours later at another one miles away without any memory of the torture.

At one point, a young Indian man had been chanting ecstatically from the sacred Hindu scriptures. Abruptly and unexpectedly, his features contorted and his eyes bulged out unnaturally while an unseen force jerked his head backward and he screamed, falling to the dirt in crippling spasms.

"What is happening to him?" I asked a bystander.

"The spirit of Kali has entered him," the man stated, "and her entrance always affects people like this."

As unsettling as this entire experience seemed, it confirmed for me much of what I had been sensing and learning, which was later reinforced by in-depth study and one-on-one ministry experiences in the United States.

## CONFRONTATIONAL MINISTRY

I began to realize that God had called me to confront the powers of darkness in an aggressive way. Even though most people try to steer clear of spiritual warfare, I became convinced that the Kingdom of God would never be able to advance unless more believers came to understand that the devil and his demons are unquestionably real and that each one of us has a personal and vital role in taking them on.

You don't have to be in a developing country to run into demons. In fact, you probably encountered some already this week as you went about your daily routines. Without expecting a "demon behind every bush," you can learn to see the demonic elements in the intractable-seeming conflicts and circumstances that occur in your life and the lives of your family and others. And you can learn to deal effectively with them.

Won't all this attention to demons create an unbalanced emphasis? Not if you take it as only one component of your spiritual experience. Set into the context of wholehearted faith (and I mean that both in terms of zeal and a wholeness of spirit and soul), the ongoing and malicious opposition of satan and his evil minions becomes just one more thing to discern and deal with.

Each of us needs to take hold of our whole calling as sons and daughters of God. Jesus calls us His own, and He has given us His authority, commanding us to do the works that He Himself did and still does (see John 14:10-12; Luke 4:18). What does that mean for us? Well, what did Jesus do?

Jesus came to Earth as a man in order to defeat the devil (who was holding the world in captivity) and to obliterate his works. The apostle John wrote, "...For this purpose the Son of God was manifested, that He might destroy the works of the devil" (1 John 3:8).

With His Spirit dwelling in our spirits, we carry on His devil-defeating work today. The same devil who was known as lucifer when he asserted himself against God and was thrown down from Heaven (see Rev. 12:7-12) is the evil one we are fighting today. Although he was defeated definitively by Jesus' death on the cross and His resurrection, he still *prowls around like a roaring lion, seeking someone to devour*" (1 Pet. 5:8 NASB).

In other words, the battle has been won already, but it has not yet been entirely enforced. Who are the enforcers? You and I are called to impose the victory of Christ on the devil and his demons.

## YOU ARE IN A BATTLE

The devil is the prince of this present age, the god of the atmosphere, and the job of driving him out is too big for just a few people. Every single Christian has an assignment in this ongoing battle.

We are in a war, like it or not. Naturally, a lot of Christians do not want to be involved. They would rather think about Heaven. They don't want to take risks or get their hands dirty. They think that if they ignore the battle that rages all around them, they won't have to get involved and that its consequences will not touch them.

But they are involved by default. The first thing you need to know is that every child of God who has confessed Jesus Christ as Lord and Savior is involved in this battle. In fact, even if you're *not* saved, you're involved simply by virtue of having been born on this planet. We are living on a battlefield where conflict rages day and night between two opposing forces.

When I was a kid, I remember riding the train. It had a cord you could pull to signal the engineer to stop. I'm sorry to have to tell you that the world we are riding on is *not* like the train; you cannot pull a cord to make it stop, and you cannot get off.

This battle between God and satan affects everything—every human being and every cultural, social, political, and moral realm of every nation on the Earth. Ceaselessly, evil battles with good, right clashes with wrong, darkness comes against the light, and the counterfeit struggles to supplant the real. The powers of the devil are not equal to the powers of God, but they take the offensive wherever they can. It's our job to put them on the defensive—and to drive them away, establishing the Kingdom of God in as many places as possible.

## SATAN IS PERSISTENT

We are fighting against the devil, who is an intelligent strategist and an obstinate fighter. He *refuses* to acknowledge defeat until he has lost everything. Even then, he will fight to get it back.

Remember the Israelites and the Promised Land. Even though God told Moses and Joshua, *"I have given you the land"* (Num. 33:53), which was stated in the past tense as an accomplished fact, Joshua and his warriors did not relax once they got there. They couldn't. They were too busy enforcing and possessing the promise. They were *fighting*. They were waging war to conquer city after city. And then they had to guard what they had conquered from being recaptured or lost.

In the same way, we must fight to possess the promises of God. We need to crumble walls in order to obtain the health and abundant provision that is on the other side. We need to lay claim to our inheritance and secure our rights. Once we win a city, we have to defend it. The enemy will never give up trying to get it back. If he fails on Monday, he will come back on Tuesday.

In all of my contending with demonic forces, I have never once heard a demon say, "You know what? You Christians are right. I'm giving up." No, they do everything up to the last second to hang onto whatever foothold they have. They wangle and fight and bargain and do not give up until they are forced to. Apparently, even though the devil realizes that Jesus' life, death, and resurrection made him a loser, he's just too proud to admit it.

## PRAYING AT ALL TIMES

We have our work cut out for us, but most people do not know how to wage this war. They think that prayer is intended to be a way to prepare for battle. But prayer is not merely preparation—prayer *is* the battle.

Paul knew this. That's why, after describing our spiritual armor in his letter to the Ephesians, he insisted that we *"pray at all times in the Spirit"* (Eph.

6:18 NASB). He also knew that we find ourselves in enemy territory from the day of our birth, so that when we start praying, we are marching into territory that already belongs to the devil. Our environment—government, culture, marketplaces of commerce and entertainment—was long ago donated to demons. No wonder the enemy works so hard to take away our prayer lives. Our prayers spell his doom.

We must accept the simple fact that we have a ruthless enemy, put on our Spirit-provided armor, and start fighting. The Bible tells us that the whole world lies in the hand of the evil one (see 1 John 5:19) and that the prince of the power of the air is the spirit that now works in the sons of disobedience (see Eph. 2:2). The Bible also says:

> For we do not wrestle against flesh and blood, but against principalities, against powers, against the rulers of the darkness of this age, against spiritual hosts of wickedness in the heavenly places (Ephesians 6:12).

The reason that some Christians have so much trouble is because they are ignorant of reality. Too many Christians go through their lives oblivious to the activities of the evil one. To them, he is an abstraction, and they seldom hear him preached about in their churches. They prefer to see the devil as a figment of human imagination, a concept left over from less sophisticated generations. Regrettably, as Hosea wrote, "*My people are destroyed for lack of knowledge...*" (Hos. 4:6).

## YOU HAVE BEEN DRAFTED

You are not a volunteer soldier in this army; you cannot choose whether or not you want to participate. You were *drafted* into the Lord's army on the day you said, "Lord Jesus, I receive You into my heart as my personal Lord and Savior." By confession of your belief in His virgin birth, His blood atonement on the cross, and His resurrection from the dead, you were conscripted for life into the army of God, like it or not. Every blood-bought believer is in this army, so you have lots of company. There is no provision for conscientious objectors.

When you were drafted into the Lord's army by your Commander-in-Chief, it's as if you suddenly switched sides. By default, you used to be on the devil's side, although you probably didn't realize it, and now you're on the Lord's side. That means that you have automatically, implicitly declared war on the devil. You don't really have a choice about it. Your only choice is whether to go AWOL or to pick up your weapons and fight. Do you want to run, or do you want to stand strong in the strength that your Commander supplies? Do you want to go absent without leave from your Commander-in-Chief, or do you want to stand up and fight in the name of Jesus?

You have been caught in crossfire—for your soul. Your decision to fight or retreat has eternal consequences. Your salvation has been secured in any case, but you don't want to enter Heaven as a cowardly soldier who hid behind others when the battle got fierce. You want to march victoriously to your eternal destination knowing that you have fought the good fight and kept the faith.

When you become a soldier in the United States Army, you sign up for conflict. The commanding officer never promises that you will be safe or never shot at. He doesn't assure you that you will never have to hurt anybody or that you'll never see any blood. Far from it. In fact, you are taught how to fight and how to use weapons. It's the same for Christian soldiers. I am glad that I'm fighting in the Lord's army. I'd rather be ducking enemy fire coming toward me than getting shot in the back running away.

Picture a young, good-looking soldier. That serviceman has been sifted and trained and tested. A recruiter didn't simply scoop him up off the street, give him a uniform, and send him straight to the front lines of battle. No, he's been thoroughly trained first. Besides being given weapons and taught how to use them, he's been trained in teamwork and loyalty and obedience. His resolve has been tested and tried. What's his commitment like? Is he willing to fight for his country to the death if necessary? Besides being drafted into the Lord's army, you have been equipped to do the fighting you will be required to do. Jesus' name alone puts terror into the hearts of His enemies. Jesus declared, *"All authority has been given to Me in heaven and on earth"* (Matt. 28:18). And His Father in Heaven:

> *...has highly exalted Him and given Him the name which is above every name, that at the name of Jesus every knee should bow, of those in heaven, and of those on earth, and of those under the earth* (Philippians 2:9-10).

## WHAT IS WARFARE PRAYER?

By invoking the name of Jesus, you are praying warfare prayer, which hinders evil operations in a place or in a person's life.

But there is a difference between spiritual warfare praying and other kinds of praying, and that difference can be seen in one particular aspect—where your prayers are directed. When the devil has invaded somebody's life, you do not pray, "Lord, if it be Your will, deliver this person from the devil." No, you look that demon in the eye and say, "In the name of Jesus, come out—now! Not tomorrow, but right *now!*" You refuse to give him in inch. Your prayers should not sound like, "Let my people go next year"; or, "Lord, would You please let my people go free?" Instead you charge the enemy himself, ordering him, "Let my people go, now!" You direct your words to the devil, and you tell him what he must do. You never tiptoe around, worried lest you offend him.

Certain prayers do not bother the devil at all, even when they are verbose, eloquent, and deep. They may sound effective, but they don't mean a hill of beans to him. Direct warfare prayers, however, really worry him. And worship (which doesn't necessarily mention the devil, because it gives honor and glory to God alone) really perturbs him.

You are there to exorcise demons, not to pretty them up. We already have too many spiritual cosmetologists in the Body of Christ, people who pray pretty prayers and put makeup on problems. What we need are warrior-surgeons who can take the Sword of the Spirit and cut out the problem in the name of Jesus.

Most Christian leaders hold back from getting involved in deliverance because they are too intimidated by their own demons (too bound and too frightened to admit it) and because they just do not know how to confront the devil. Nobody explained spiritual warfare to them in Bible school or seminary. Or even if it was explained, they missed the part about Jesus' authority—which is significantly weakened if a person has unrepented-of sin in his or her life. When you get involved in deliverance and you are practicing hanky-panky on the side, the devil is going to call your bluff. You have to walk the talk, live the life, and be bold with both the authority and power of Jesus Christ, bold enough to march into the jaws of hell, look the devil in the eye, tell him he is a loser, order him to get out now, and insist that you will never take "no" for an answer.

## DOING WHAT JESUS DID

I have devoted my whole ministry to praying warfare prayers. Yet I don't want people to rely on me or any other expert to get the job done. I want everybody to know how to pray against the devil successfully.

The Gospels record time after time when Jesus delivered people from unclean spirits—and commissioned the disciples to do so too. He taught them what they would need to know in order to combat the enemy of their souls. If you never thought about it before, just open your Bible and read Matthew 16:19; 25:41; Mark 1:12-13;23-28,34,39; 3:14-15; 6:7; Luke 4:1-13, 33-35; 10:17-20; and John 8:44-49. Jesus and His followers were confronting the devil at every turn.

Understanding how the devil robs and harms people gives fresh meaning to Jesus' story of the Good Samaritan (see Luke 10:30-37). After the man who had been robbed and beaten got bypassed by both a priest and a Levite, an ordinary Samaritan man came by and took it upon himself to help the victim. Jesus told this story, and then He said to His followers, "*Go and do likewise*" (Luke 10:37). That's what He's telling us to do, too.

I teach and pray about this fulltime because I want as many people as possible to be true disciples and true spiritual warriors. This book is my concerted attempt to remedy the lack of bold faith and prayer within the Body of Christ and to mobilize more foot soldiers across the face of the Earth. In this book, I will lay out ten life lessons for becoming a successful spiritual warrior, along with ten corresponding prayers and proclamations that you will be able to use effectively.

You and I fight shoulder-to-shoulder in the Lord's army. Let's pray and persist in this cosmic war until the end of our time on Earth.

# PART I
# LIFE LESSONS

Ten Life Lessons for
Becoming a Spiritual Warrior

# Chapter 1

# Your Destiny: Seizing the Reason You Are Here

*Life Lesson #1: Be a Winner, Not a Whiner*

ALL day long, wherever He went, Jesus ministered to people. As He walked from place to place with His disciples, He spent His time teaching about the Kingdom of God and taking care of the needs of the people: healing them, raising the dead, casting out demons, and more. He was very busy, and yet He seemed to move around from place to place without a set schedule or itinerary.

Then suddenly one day He *"set His face to go to Jerusalem."* Abruptly He had a destination and a timetable. Nothing could deter Him.

> *Now it came to pass, when the time had come for Him to be received up, that He steadfastly set His face to go to Jerusalem, and sent messengers before His face. And as they went, they entered a village of the Samaritans, to prepare for Him. But they did not receive Him, because His face was set for the journey to Jerusalem (Luke 9:51-53).*

His face was set for the journey to Jerusalem. He didn't need a map or a GPS to point Him there. He knew where He was going. More than that, He had lived every moment of His adult life already knowing that the time would come when He would set His face to go to Jerusalem, and He already knew what would happen there. As He *"went about doing good"* (Acts 10:38) in the countryside around Jerusalem, He was fully aware of what the last chapter of His earthly life would look like. He knew what He was called to do and even what specific city to go to. He knew His exact purpose and destiny.

It seemed as though He had scarcely begun to minister to the massive needs of the people of the region, and yet He knew when the time was right for Him to travel to the city of Jerusalem. There He would be arrested, get convicted of crimes He had not committed, and be tortured and crucified. His preaching and His works of healing and deliverance were just a taste of the victory to come. Jesus' destiny was to destroy the works of the devil, and He paved the way for the rest of us to enforce His victory.

Jesus was faithful and steadfast to His calling, in spite of the fact that it entailed greater suffering than anyone had ever endured before. Nothing changed His mind. And once He had set His face toward the city of Jerusalem, nothing else mattered to Him except getting there and accomplishing each of the appointed tasks.

Sometimes we talk about "divine appointments." Jesus' destiny—to go to Calvary and die on the cross for the sins of the world—was the most divine appointment of all time! He showed us how to be on time for our own divine appointments and how to carry them through.

## YOU HAVE A DESTINY

Each of us, although we are not as likely to understand our calling as Jesus was, has been created with a divinely appointed destiny. You and I too have our "Jerusalem," and we must set our determination like iron to follow God's will to the end. Besides acknowledging the lordship of Jesus, who went before us to His Jerusalem, where He won for us our freedom, we rely on His Holy Spirit to guide us and protect us as we direct our steps unfalteringly to an unseen goal.

Do we do this very well?

No we don't, sad to say. In fact, most Christians today respond to just about everything *except* their destiny, and if they have a glimmering of an idea about what their destiny entails, they become frightened and hesitant. They second-guess themselves and fall prey to what can only be called the "spirit of our age."

Instead of seizing the time and plotting a divinely inspired course toward their calling, they are marking time or biding time, hoping that things won't get too horrible, praying mostly for comfort and agreeable circumstances. As a result—no surprise here—their chance to fulfill their God-given destiny either passes them by or remains constantly out of their reach. Their diverted destiny becomes a dream or a distant hope rather than a daily and passionate pursuit.

## WHAT STANDS IN THE WAY?

Life circumstances seem to conspire against us. Many of us are simply overwhelmed much of the time. In a recent survey, Americans who professed to be born-again Christians described their lives. Of this sampling of typical people, 31 percent said they were "stressed out." Almost half of them, 49 percent, said they were "too busy." Many of those same people, 40 percent of the total number, were in financial debt, while 11 percent were dealing with addiction. Almost half described themselves as "searching for purpose." They acknowledged that they were Christians, and yet they were failing to grasp even the beginning of an idea about their purpose in life.

I do not need to tell you that life today has become highly complex. Our cell phones and other types of electronic devices do not really save us any time or trouble. Demands pull us in many different directions. Confronted with many choices, some of them life-altering in their importance, we fail to consult God for guidance. And the more choices we are faced with, the more likely it is that we will eventually make bad choices. As a result, many people—perhaps most people—become neutralized, simply reacting to the latest crisis as best they can.

Some of the choices that face us can be labeled as temptations, and yet we are confronted with so many of them we get used to them. We become accustomed to a daily barrage of distractions. Such persistent and insistent distractions represent temptations that detour us from our personal destinies.

The company we keep does not very often help us "set our face to Jerusalem." Regardless of whether we examine our employment, our friendships, or even our marriages, the people around us do not seem to see much need for long-term loyalty to anything. This dearth of loyalty has infiltrated many people's faith. How can we remain committed to a God-given destiny when everybody around us undermines commitment in the first place?

## HOW TO BE A WHINER

Not only are we distracted from our goals and diffused in our commitments, most of us also slip into "poor me" mode from time to time. Some, in fact, have raised whining and complaining to an art form.

You are in the break room at work. Other people are there, too. Some are reading magazines or looking at their E-mails. What kinds of comments do you hear—and say? Most likely, grumbling, mumbling, complaining, and whining ones. It's been a rough day, after all. Everyone else is complaining about their circumstances, so why not join the crowd?

Why not make your attitude contingent upon your circumstances? Why not refuse to act upbeat until you have all your ducks lined up in a neat little row? Why not let the world know how dissatisfied you will be until your circumstances conform to your personal desires? "When I close this deal, then I'll be happy." "When I get married, then I'll be happy." "When I get that overtime pay, then I'll be happy." "Until X happens, I intend to act sour and cynical."

I'm sure you will be exceedingly happy when your ship finally comes in. But if you adopt that whiner mentality, most likely you will miss happiness when it finally arrives, having wasted your life chasing one meaningless thing after another. As an added bonus, you'll be a miserable person to be around, and people will steer clear of you.

Whiners are worriers, too. They specialize in contemplating worst-case scenarios. "What if I get sick?" "What if I lose my job?" Of course, most of the things you worry about will never happen anyway, but make sure you play them out in your mind. Turn them over and over again on the rotisserie grill of your emotions. Religious worriers will listen to the latest prophetic prediction of disaster and let that drive them into a foxhole of fear.

Fear, worry, and complaining together comprise unbelief, don't they? And Christian *un*believers are all too common. One of the telltale signs of this kind of person is tightfistedness, at least when it comes to God's work. These people may appear to be generous, but their generosity is on their own terms. When they give money or resources to God's work, they make sure they give out of their surplus, after they have spent all they want on themselves. They tithe on their leftovers, not on their firstfruits. For them, stewardship is a heavy burden, and they are not shy about complaining to other Christians about it.

## HOW TO BE A WINNER

What does whining versus winning have to do with spiritual warfare? It has everything to do with attitude, and no warrior will get very far with a "poor me" frame of reference. In order to be a winning spiritual warrior, you must ditch your self-centeredness and exchange it for a life that is sold out for God.

How? For starters, by following these three Cs, which will keep your own "road to Jerusalem" wide open before you:

1.  Consistently cleanse your life. Daily, just as you look in the mirror to check your face and clothing, look in the mirror of the Word to find out if you can see your reflection in it.

Make adjustments according to what the Bible tells you. You are supposed to *"put on the Lord Jesus Christ"* (Rom. 13:14), which means clothing your character with His purity.

2. Constantly confess your sins. When you see that you have missed the mark, deal with it right away. By dealing with your "issues" as they arise, you remove every hindrance to pursuing your destiny. This is the key to keeping spiritually fit and strong:

   *Therefore, since we are surrounded by such a huge crowd of witnesses to the life of faith, let us strip off every weight that slows us down, especially the sin that so easily trips us up. And let us run with endurance the race God has set before us. We do this by keeping our eyes on Jesus, the champion who initiates and perfects our faith. Because of the joy awaiting Him, He endured the cross, disregarding its shame. Now He is seated in the place of honor beside God's throne. Think of all the hostility He endured from sinful people; then you won't become weary and give up* (Hebrews 12:1-3 NLT).

3. Courageously commit your life to Jesus Christ. Christians who are winners are spiritual warriors, and warriors are willing to make whatever sacrifice might be necessary to follow their Savior. They willingly lay down their lives for the One who laid down His life for them. In what ways is God calling you to lay down your life today?

## TEARING DOWN STRONGHOLDS

Some people are so scared of the devil that they think merely saying his name gives him some kind of power over them. They think that if they get around spiritual warfare and demons, something is going to jump out of the dark and nab them. I tell them, "You may smell his breath, but he can't get you if you don't give him any opening." The devil does not land anywhere he's not welcome. If he lands on you, then you need to look for some area of your life that has given him access.

All of our "issues" separate us from God. They are sinful. Worse than that, they can create strongholds in our lives; strongholds are pockets of sinfulness that provide cover for the devil to operate "behind the lines" and interfere with everything we do.

The only stronghold you want in your life is the stronghold of Jesus Christ Himself.

> The LORD is my rock and my fortress and my deliverer; my God, my strength, in whom I will trust; my shield and the horn of my salvation, my **stronghold** (Psalm 18:2).

All other strongholds need to be demolished.

One of the first things you should do as you set your face toward your destiny is to ask God to show you your own strongholds. Everybody's got some junk inside, so it's nothing to be ashamed of. Jesus came to save us from everything that holds us captive, including our internal "stuff." Even when the enemy tries to make you feel guilty about things in your past, you don't have to give him the time of day. He's the accuser of the brethren, and you are one of the brethren now.

Jesus never makes you feel guilty and condemned:

> There is therefore now no condemnation to those who are in Christ Jesus, who do not walk according to the flesh, but according to the Spirit (Romans 8:1).

*...Now salvation, and strength, and the kingdom of our God, and the power of His Christ have come, for the accuser of our brethren, who accused them before our God day and night, has been cast down* (Revelation 12:10).

What kind of thing will you be looking for?

A stronghold is not a demon, although demons can take advantage of their existence. Neither is it a specific sin or even an erroneous belief, although both contribute to the strength of a stronghold.

A stronghold is anything you rely upon to defend yourself other than the Lord Himself. The Pharisees had many doctrinal and cultural strongholds, and Jesus was not afraid to take them to task for them. Some strongholds are pretty to look at, and some are ugly—although all of them are invisible to the human eye. They are internal structures of unsanctified feelings and thoughts, and they affect everything you do. A stronghold is a place of emotional invest- ment in your life. Satan intensifies that emotion until it's over the edge and controls your actions.

Strongholds welcome darkness and evil into your life, but they are not the same as what I technically call a "legal right." The difference between strong- holds and legal rights is simple: a legal right is how the devil gets in. The stronghold is how he stays in. (I am defining "in" very broadly. I mean any kind of attack, oppression, or torment of the enemy—some kind of access to your life.) You can remove a legal right by repentance and renunciation, and it needs to happen first, before you determine to pull down the stronghold.

A legal right is sinful behavior that has not been repented of. Whether someone has committed an open act of violent murder or is holding onto and hiding an unforgiving heart, any unrepented-of sin is like an open door to the enemy. If you ever dabbled in the occult, for instance—even in a limited way such as playing with an Ouija board or calling a psychic hotline—you com- mitted a willful and deliberate sin against God, and you put your trust in His enemy's power. Ever since, the devil has had a legal right to be involved in your life. In fact, you gave him a handshake and welcomed him in.

Wait—when you got saved, didn't that erase those legal rights? Didn't all your sins get washed away? Wasn't that a fresh start? No, it was not an automatic clean slate. Becoming a Christian did save your soul, and it brought you into a right relationship with Jesus Christ. But if you ever engaged the enemy in some way, even informally, that agreement remains in force over the circumstances of your life until you do something about it. You will still go to Heaven. You haven't sold your soul to the devil. But your feet will be entangled, and your life-journey will be filled with detours. Your destiny will always remain out of your grasp.

You want to disentangle yourself as soon as possible, so that you can get on the winning track toward your destiny.

## STEP ONE: BREAK OFF SATAN'S LEGAL ACCESS

The devil is very legalistic. When he came before the throne of God to attack Job (see Job 1), he did not have a legal right to attack Job. He was looking for a legal right. Just as he does with us, he was looking for a loophole.

Once a legal right gets established and the devil gains access to your life, he starts looking around for something to feed on. He may see some unhealed rejection. So even though he cannot rob you of your ultimate salvation, he can make your life a hell on earth, filled with rejection and pain. Far from being a winning spiritual warrior, you will remain a whining spiritual wimp.

You can break off the legal access, though, and it's not a complicated process. To break off satan's legal access to your life, you need to determine the sin you need to renounce and repent of. Even if it was your parents' sin, you can renounce and repent of it. (Your parents' authority over your life gave them what we call "spiritual power of attorney," and their decisions can allow evil into your life.)

Renouncing and repenting means that you turn away from a sin and declare that you will never do it again. You say, "This is something I want to be free from." You then make steps to modify your behavior in the future. If you can successfully modify your behavior and correct it by adopting right thinking and making right choices, that is all you need to do.

## DEMOLITION TIME

But if you find yourself hitting some kind of a wall when you try to stay free of that particular sin, when you have tried to get fixed and you cannot stay fixed no matter how much you pray and read your Bible, then you may be dealing with something more entrenched—a stronghold.

A demonic stronghold is different from human immaturity. You can grow out of immaturity, but you can never grow out of a stronghold. A young Christian may not have graduated from milk to meat yet, and as a result lots of things in his life may still be "off," but many of those things will resolve themselves over time as the process of sanctification proceeds.

A stronghold, on the other hand, has a deep grip on a person's psyche. When a person comes into a situation that triggers a negative internal reaction that is too intense to be managed by quoting a Bible verse or calling on the Lord for help, then most likely the person is dealing with a stronghold. It is a supernatural impediment, and it requires the application of supernatural weapons:

> *For though we walk in the flesh, we do not war according to the flesh. For the weapons of our warfare are not carnal but mighty in God for pulling down strongholds, casting down arguments and every high thing that exalts itself against the knowledge of God, bringing every thought into captivity to the obedience of Christ* (2 Corinthians 10:3-5).

The first of those supernatural weapons is basic repentance, along with confession and renunciation. This removes the legal access that has given the devil a foothold in your life. For example, if you are having trouble with anger that stems from unforgiveness in your heart, you must decide to forgive, speak out your forgiveness (even if the person you are forgiving has died and you are speaking to thin air), and ask God to help you bless that person instead. After repenting of your unforgiveness, which was one of the doorways by which the evil one gained legal entry into your life, you take stock of your situation. Are you still having trouble with out-of-control anger?

If so, next you need to wage war on the supernatural forces that still hang onto your emotions, intensifying them and making them explosive. In other words, you need to pull down a stronghold of anger.

This is easy *not* to do, because it can be difficult, especially if you do not have help. Members of the Body of Christ who are more mature and free than you are should be able to help you pull down your strongholds. Unfortunately, most of the Body of Christ does not have a clue about what a stronghold is. Your brothers and sisters in Christ will tell you to pray longer, to fast, to read your Bible, to try everything except the one thing that will work: looking to Jesus, the pioneer and perfecter of our faith (see Heb. 12:2) and doing whatever He tells you to do.

Jesus' Spirit will help you discern the difference between an actual stronghold and the smoke screens that satan blows in your face. He will help you decide that something in your life is truly uncontrollable and in need of supernatural help. He will show you the difference between different kinds of strongholds so that you can deal with them individually.

And He will help you personally and individually address each stronghold by name, saying something like, "In the name of Jesus and as a child of God I take authority over the spiritual forces of darkness that are attacking me through the stronghold of fear/anger/rejection (or whatever else), and I pull that stronghold down, brick by brick. I apply the principle of binding and loosing (see Matt. 18:18), and I bind the powers of darkness in my life, while

I loose the power of the Holy Spirit to bring love, joy, and peace to my heart." If you have somebody to help you pray, so much the better, since where two or more agree in prayer, more power is released (see the next verse, Matthew 18:19).

By intentionally praying this way, you will have pulled down that stronghold. You are free now. However, you are going to have to hold your ground. You're still going to have to keep doing the right things and repenting of more sin. You would be wise to keep involving yourself in healthy Christian activities, reading your Bible, and going to church. You want to replace the former stronghold with the Stronghold of your Savior.

## THE MOST COMMON STRONGHOLDS

I have spent decades ministering spiritual freedom and inner healing to people, and I've discovered thousands, perhaps millions, of strongholds that the devil exploits. But the most common ones fall into six categories: (1) fear, (2) anger, (3) rejection, (4) depression, (5) self-hatred, and (6) abuse. As you can see, each of these categories represents an area in which the emotions can be attacked. If satan has set up housekeeping in that part of your life, it's as if he owns that emotion.

Too often, people brush off the seriousness of their strongholds, even when they can identify them. "Well," they say, "that's just the way I am. My mom was that way; my uncle is that way." They convince themselves that they are unlikely to get free. Or they say, "Well, it doesn't seem too demonic. It just seems like normal emotional reactions to life. I don't need to call it a fancy word like *stronghold*. I'm just hurting."

Satan runs a stealth operation. Of course he doesn't want people to know they have strongholds. Do you think he will advertise his handiwork? I don't think so. You will never see him popping up to shout, "See! Here I am! Come and get rid of me!" He knows you will leave him alone if you think your chronic emotional and relational problems are your own fault, or that you can blame them on your parents. He also knows you will leave him alone if you feel ashamed of your behavior, so he makes sure you feel vulnerable and fearful about sharing your need with others.

The devil will lie to you. He will say, "You are a Christian, so you should be able to handle this." Sure enough, you tried putting it at Jesus' feet, but it seems to jump back into your life, and you're still wrestling with it. Yet instead of saying to your Christian friends, "Guess what? I'm still struggling. Can you come around me and help strengthen me?" you run from it even more. You can't deal with it, so you hide your weakness and pretend that you are free.

If you had a broken foot, you would go to the doctor and get a cast put on it. Your pain would force you to do that. By the same token, your internal pain should force you to find help. You *are* weak, and you do need Jesus to be your strength. But you are so weak that you end up failing to get the help you need because you are unable to admit it to someone.

Quit making excuses and stop living in denial. You have a problem, and you need help. The Bible puts it this way: Confess your faults one to another, and you will be healed (see James 5:16).

## GETTING HELP

You can't pull down your strongholds by yourself. Let's say you have a problem with a satanic stronghold of self-hatred. You despise yourself. You also know that Jesus said, "*Love your neighbor as yourself*" (see Matt. 19:19; Mark 12:31; Luke 10:27). There's only one problem: You *can't* love your neighbor because you don't even love yourself. You can't have positive and healthy relationships, because you hate who you are. You are carrying a stronghold of self-hatred, and you keep feeding on it. Self-hatred is messing with your psyche, your feelings, your mind, your thought processes. You have already tried to take care of it yourself, but you ended up feeling worse. You feel stuck.

Finally, in desperation, you seek out someone in the Body of Christ who knows about strongholds. You tell that person that you have a real problem with self-hatred and that in fact you are in bondage to it. You tell him or her that you want to pull that stronghold down and dismantle it, because you want to have spiritual freedom.

Then that person (or group of persons) speaks truth to your spirit. Speaking to you by name, they say, "I/we love you. We are sorry that you have grown to hate yourself, but we love you no matter what, unconditionally. We are going to battle for you in the name and authority of Jesus. Spirit of self-hatred, you do not have a right to control our friend. Be gone from his/her life right now. We completely dismantle the stronghold of self-hatred. Self-hatred no longer has validity in this life...."

You achieve freedom by allowing someone to minister to you such as a pastor, priest, a Christian mental health professional, or some other caring trained person, someone skilled to know how to reach the hidden strongholds and touch the part of your life that you do not know how to touch. (Our ministry has scores of Do What Jesus Did, DWJD®, deliverance teams located worldwide. Simply contact our offices at www.boblarson.org for a referral.)

Alone, your chances of being able to pull down a personal stronghold are very slim. By yourself, you are too disabled by the very issue to take authority over it, at least at first. With help, you can make that prayer your own, and you can break free from the stronghold of self-hatred. You can walk out of that jail.

And yet you will continue to need the support of your brothers and sisters in Christ as you re-learn how to love. You will need lots of coaching and lots of practice. You cannot coach yourself, and you cannot practice by yourself. In fact, you may find it hard to remember that you are no longer the same person. You may indeed have stepped free of a stronghold, but you are not automatically knowledgeable about how to walk in freedom.

## STANDING IN THE WINNER'S CIRCLE

Your goal is to reach your Jerusalem, where your destiny can be fulfilled. Before you battle your way forward past external foes and obstacles, you need to vanquish internal enemies, who often occupy strongholds deep inside your being. Before you can complete your journey and stand in the winner's circle, you need to join yourself to others who are on the same road. Like a heavenly army, you can move forward together toward the ultimate goal—winning more souls and more territory for the Kingdom of God. Helping each other, we all become winners.

Winners allow their weakness to be turned into strength. They look to Jesus' example. When He set His face toward Jerusalem, He did not let encumbrances entangle His feet. Neither can you.

> *Therefore, since we have so great a cloud of witnesses surrounding us, let us also lay aside every encumbrance and the sin which so easily entangles us, and let us run with endurance the race that is set before us, fixing our eyes on Jesus, the author and perfecter of faith, who for the joy set before Him endured the cross, despising the shame, and has sat down at the right hand of the throne of God* (Hebrews 12:1-2 NASB).

Go into battle with the attitude, I'm a winner, not a whiner. Satan's a loser; he is defeated. I am more than a conqueror with and for Jesus Christ.

# Chapter 2

# Your Calling: Standing Firm Like David

*Life Lesson #2: Be a Warrior, Not a Wimp*

E was nine feet, nine inches tall, and his bronze helmet and scale armor weighed 125 pounds. He carried a bronze sword and an oversized spear as big as a weaver's beam; the iron spear-tip alone weighed at least 15 pounds. As he strode from place to place, shaking the earth with each step, his shield-bearer, a strong warrior in his own right, preceded him.

You know who this is. I am describing Goliath, whose very name has become synonymous with arrogant antagonism. (See First Samuel 17:4-7.) Yet his name would not be remembered at all if a ruddy-faced youth called David had not confronted him with his simple slingshot.

David had come to bring lunch to his older brothers on the battlefield when he first heard of this intimidating Philistine named Goliath. The army of Israel was quaking in their sandals when the giant mocked them and roared his challenge:

> *Then he stood and cried out to the armies of Israel, and said to them, "Why have you come out to line up for battle? Am I not a Philistine, and you the servants of Saul? Choose a man for yourselves, and let him come down to me. If he is able to fight with me and kill me, then we will be your servants. But if I prevail*

*against him and kill him, then you shall be our servants and serve us." And the Philistine said, "I defy the armies of Israel this day; give me a man, that we may fight together." When Saul and all Israel heard these words of the Philistine, they were dismayed and greatly afraid* (1 Samuel 17:8-11).

David, who was used to being the sole protector of his father's sheep and who had confronted attacking lions and bears by himself, was ready for the challenge. If these grown men were so terrified that they could not even open their mouths in reply to Goliath, he was going to find a way to step up and fight himself. Who else was going to do it? He could not let fear cripple his resolve. He would not allow doubt into his mind. David recognized that the living God, whom Goliath had defied, would fight with him:

*Then David spoke to the men who stood by him, saying, "What shall be done for the man who kills this Philistine and takes away the reproach from Israel? For who is this uncircumcised Philistine, that he should defy the armies of the living God?" And the people answered him in this manner, saying, "So shall it be done for the man who kills him." Now Eliab his oldest brother heard when he spoke to the men; and Eliab's anger was aroused against David, and he said, "Why did you come down here? And with whom have you left those few sheep in the wilderness? I know your pride and the insolence of your heart, for you have come down to see the battle"* (1 Samuel 17:26-28).

David did not allow even his brother's insulting retort to breed self-doubt or self-condemnation. He simply went for it—and won not only the battle, but an enduring place in the history of God's people. That day, fortified by the Lord God, to whom he had written psalms while he tended his father's sheep, he stepped forward to meet his destiny and the calling for which he had been created.

## WIMPY WARRIORS

The rest of those fighting men turned out to be wimps (although you won't find that word in the Bible account!). Yet their response seems somewhat excusable. Was it not reasonable to stay safe? King Saul had not ordered any of them to take Goliath's challenge. Surely that meant they were exempt, at least for the moment, from risking their lives so foolishly.

These grown men may have been part of a standing army, but they were wimpy warriors because of three factors: (1) the intimidation of the enemy, (2) self-doubt, and (3) self-condemnation. They did not think they would win. They forgot about God.

David didn't forget. That's why he said, *"Who is this uncircumcised Philistine, that he should defy the armies of the living God?"* And that's why one of King Saul's servants said, *"Look, I have seen a son of Jesse the Bethlehemite, who is skillful in playing, a mighty man of valor, a man of war, prudent in speech, and a handsome person; and the* LORD *is with him"* (1 Sam. 16:18).

God is bigger than any enemy, and true warriors—I mean spiritual warriors now—never forget that fact. Even though the shepherd David was a mere lyre-playing youth, he knew that his real strength came straight from God. This confidence made him able to prevail against a truly formidable military foe. In every case, only God's strength can sweep us to victory against unseen, spiritual forces of evil. His supernatural might can make even the weakest Christian a powerhouse of spiritual strength.

## CHRISTIAN SISSIES?

The modern world is full of supervisors, managers, administrators, and executives, but very few warriors (outside of the national armed services). That puts us at a disadvantage. We don't have much of a concept of what a warrior is like, nor do we have an appreciation for soldierly behavior. For lots of good reasons, we value peace-making and compromise. But the main spiritual result produced by our compromising ways is that we do not know how to fight and win the great battles of the human soul. Both the world and the Body of Christ desperately need real warriors who know how to engage in ultimate, extreme, eternal battles.

Too often the followers of Christ are portrayed as the wimpiest individuals of all, spiritual geeks wearing dark-rimmed glasses and pocket-protectors, softies both physically and spiritually who subscribe to nonviolence—even when confronted by a malevolent devil. In the name of a "gentle Jesus, meek and mild," they prefer to allow somebody else to get their hands dirty fighting.

What it comes down to is that they don't know the real Jesus at all. Jesus is a warrior and He has commissioned us as spiritual warriors too. He is our Commander-in-Chief who has conscripted us for spiritual warfare.

True warriors are bold. They step up to meet every challenge. True warriors have left their legacy throughout history. They have been rich or poor, learned or unlearned, trained or untrained. They have come from every race, language, and culture of the world. Some sought the spotlight, while many had no ambition to be judged great or to become renowned. Most were ordinary people who were victims of circumstances, violent circumstances that put demands on the hidden qualities of their character. A few were driven to fight by personal, passionate goals.

Whether or not the great historical warriors were conscripted soldiers or willing volunteers, they were prepared to fight until their particular battle was won. In every age, true warriors consider defeats to be only temporary setbacks, and struggles spur them on to greater efforts.

It's time for the world to find out that the Body of Christ is an army of true warriors who fight relentlessly against an insidious foe.

## TRAINING FOR THE WAR

When people undertake military training, they learn basic strategies and techniques, some of it from books and in classrooms, but much of it by means of hands-on practice. In fact, any amount of book-learning is useless without practical application.

In the case of Christian warriors, the Bible is our training manual, and daily life provides us with plenty of practice. Ordinary events become our boot camp and our target range. Daily life teaches us to assemble and maintain our weapons. Our rehearsals prepare us for action.

That's how it worked for David. His long days and nights tending his father's sheep had provided him with plenty of preparation for taking on Goliath, although he had to persuade Saul that he knew what he was doing:

> David said to Saul, "Let no one lose heart on account of this Philistine; your servant will go and fight him." Saul replied, "You are not able to go out against this Philistine and fight him; you are only a boy, and he has been a fighting man from his youth." But David said to Saul, "Your servant has been keeping his father's sheep. When a lion or a bear came and carried off a sheep from the flock, I went after it, struck it and rescued the sheep from its mouth. When it turned on me, I seized it by its hair, struck it and killed it. Your servant has killed both the lion and the bear; this uncircumcised Philistine will be like one of them, because he has defied the armies of the living God. The Lord who delivered me from the paw of the lion and the paw of the bear will deliver me from the hand of this Philistine." Saul said to David, "Go, and the Lord be with you" (1 Samuel 17:32-37 NIV).

David, you see, had learned how to *go after* an enemy. He had learned that successful defensive action involves aggressive offensive action. He didn't wait for somebody else to take care of things. He not only rescued the sheep that were being victimized by the predator, he grabbed attacking lions with his bare hands and put them out of commission.

His experiences in the sheep pastures made him view Goliath as a predatory lion, and he had the courage and boldness to take him on in one-on-one combat. We tend to minimize its importance, but in fact outright aggression plays a vital role in our spiritual battles.

I'm grateful for anybody who will minister healing and deliverance, but I find that some people minister what I call "Deliverance Lite." They murmur a prayer for healing and then expect that the devil will "just go away" now, in Jesus' name, amen. Do you think that works? Simply because he's been shown the door, the enemy of our souls will not exit gracefully. Satan will not give an inch unless he's hunted down, persistently.

Like David, we need to put pressure on our Goliaths as soon as we find out about them. We can't afford to wait. The passage of time will not solve the problem; it will only get worse and worse.

We can't wait until the devil is inside the front door. We need to start fighting now. Sometimes parents come to me and say, "Deliver my child." They don't understand that they are partly at fault. They are the ones who let the lion and the bear in the front door in the form of the unsupervised video games, movies, television, music, and so on. And now they want me to kick the devil out of their family? They have welcomed all kinds of evil into their home instead of seizing them by the hair as David did. They need to become more spiritually vigilant themselves before they resort to outside help.

Those who are spiritually successful in battle get to their troubles before their troubles get to them. Or, as I tell people all over the world, "Get your stuff before your stuff gets you. Get your demons before your demons get you."

Never start your training in the midst of the battle. How dumb would it be to send a raw recruit into a battlefield when the bullets are flying, and then hand him a boot camp manual? Sometimes we do the spiritual equivalent.

People come for ministry, desperate. "I need help. Satan is attacking me." We ask them where they go to church. "Well, I don't go anywhere right now." In fact, in most cases they haven't gone anywhere for a long time. They're not reading their Bible. They're not praying. As a result, they were not in a position to deal with their troubles while they were still manageable. They weren't building up their spiritual muscles. The next thing you know, they've become a casualty of accumulated "stuff," and they want me, or you, to perform a miraculous cure or a one-size-fits-all deliverance.

Always underlying our training and motivating us to vigilance are three essential facts: *The enemy is powerful.* He is not more powerful than God Himself, but he is definitely no wimp. His malice motivates him to attack on many fronts, some obvious and some subtle. Sometimes what you call a "bad day" or blame on unkind people is really a heavy undercover assault from the devil. *Our authority is unlimited.* All power under Heaven has been given to Christ Jesus, and He has commissioned us to use the authority of His name wherever we go. *The consequences are eternal.* We do not fight spiritual battles in order to improve our quality of life for only a day or a week or a month, but rather to affect the destiny of souls for ever and ever.

We need to develop a warrior's mindset that will keep us on the alert at all times.

## ANTICIPATING ENEMY TACTICS

Remember, by definition, the devil is a liar. He accuses. He insinuates. He undermines. He knows full well that the best way to begin to destroy is to disturb our composure, to rattle us up.

"The accuser of the brethren" is his job description. Relentlessly, he accuses believers of trumped-up charges. In his great vision of Heaven, John saw this and recorded it in the Book of Revelation:

*And the great dragon was thrown down, the serpent of old who is called the devil and Satan, who deceives the whole world; he was thrown down to the earth, and his angels were thrown down with him. Then I heard a loud voice in heaven, saying, "Now the salvation, and the power, and the kingdom of our God and the authority of His Christ have come, for the **accuser of our brethren** has been thrown down, he **who accuses them before our God day and night**"* (Revelation 12:9-10 NASB).

Satan often uses human beings to perpetrate his lies. Jesus addressed those who were collaborating with the evil one. He spoke harshly to the Pharisees and diagnosed their evil motivations:

*You belong to your father, the devil, and you want to carry out your father's desire. He was a murderer from the beginning, not holding to the truth, for there is no truth in him. When he lies, he speaks his native language, for he is a liar and the father of lies* (John 8:44 NIV).

The devil is a liar. He has always been a liar, and he always will be a liar. That doesn't mean he doesn't sometimes resort to the truth—which he will subtly mix with a lie so that you can't figure it out, as he did with Eve in Eden:

*"...Did God really say you must not eat the fruit from any of the trees in the garden?" "Of course we may eat fruit from the trees in the garden," the woman replied. "It's only the fruit from the tree in the middle of the garden that we are not allowed to eat..."* (Genesis 3:1-3 NLT).

Continually, the enemy charges Christians with false crimes, offenses, lapses of judgment, errors, perceived sins, and failure of all kinds—based on actual events. Needless to say, his accusations are not meant to help you out of your sins. The devil is in the business of making people feel guilty in order to incapacitate them.

He has an armory full of accusations. For example: "You don't pray enough," or "You pray too much." (Either way, he makes the time you spend with the Lord insignificant because you're never satisfied with your spiritual life.) "You don't read the Bible enough," or "You read the Bible too much." He'll chide you for your lack of biblical knowledge, or he'll condemn you for bibliolatry—worshiping the Bible. He'll trap you between the guilt of neglect and the fear of obsession, always looking for a Scripture for every single move you make.

Here's one of the enemy's favorite lines: "You aren't pleasing God if you fall short of His expectations." It plays straight into our confusion between God's expectations and our own expectations. Too many of us carry around a faulty works-driven desire to perform well enough for God to love us. This makes us fall prey to accusations about the validity of our salvation. Satan wants to keep you off balance. He wants you to question whether you're good enough for God's Kingdom. He wants you to worry that you won't finish well. The Word has a rebuttal to that accusation: *Being confident of this very thing, that He who has begun a good work in you will complete it until the day of Jesus Christ"* (Phil. 1:6).

The enemy's tactics are designed to affect your mind and emotions. He can't possess your spirit, which belongs to God for eternity, but he hounds your soul relentlessly. Your soul includes your thoughts, your feelings, your emotions, your aversions, and your passions. The devil is like an insurgent who wages war on civilians and soldiers alike. Like a terrorist, he doesn't care who he blows up. He plants explosive devices where people least expect them. You need to be vigilant: *"Stay alert! Watch out for your great enemy, the devil. He prowls around like a roaring lion, looking for someone to devour"* (1 Pet. 5:8 NLT).

Like good soldiers, spiritual warriors put body armor on the most vulnerable places, and that means guarding their minds and emotions at all times. They do not leave their helmets of salvation or their breastplates of righteousness at home! They know that their mental activity produces ideas that are the building blocks of decisions and that if the devil stages an attack on their minds, he can snare them. Jesus warned us against lustful thoughts (see Matt. 5:28). He said, *"Out of the heart proceed evil thoughts, murders, adulteries, fornications, thefts, false witness, blasphemies"* (Matt. 15:19).

Along with evil thoughts come feelings. Satan wants to invade your every state of conscious awareness: your sentiments, your convictions, your attitudes, your opinions, and your emotional reactions. If he can't capture you by means of your thoughts, he will ambush your feelings. Paul referred to this tactic when he admonished the Ephesian church not to walk as the Gentiles walk: *"Who, being past feeling, have given themselves over to lewdness, to work all uncleanness with greediness"* (Eph. 4:19).

What can you do in the face of such an assault? Your ability to wage war against the evil one is directly related to your ability to distinguish truth from error. Paul told Timothy that a mature and committed Christian is *"a workman who does not need to be ashamed, accurately handling the word of truth"* (2 Tim. 2:15 NASB). A spiritual warrior can be no less and ought to be more.

Warriors guard their souls. They weigh their thoughts carefully, subjecting them to God's scrutiny, *"casting down arguments and every high thing that exalts itself against the knowledge of God, bringing every thought into captivity to the obedience of Christ"* (2 Cor. 10:5). Spiritual warriors gauge their feelings by the Word of God, and they temper their emotions by the Holy Spirit.

## DEFINING A WARRIOR

Besides alertness to potential assaults and attention to spiritual armor, what else defines a true warrior in God's army? I can think of five distinguishing features, in brief, as follows: (1) A warrior is never focused on fear. (2) A warrior is right with God. (3) A warrior knows how to fight on any battlefield. (4) A warrior knows what he is fighting for. (5) A warrior knows that losing is not an option. Let's explore these, so that we can assess our personal fitness to be spiritual combatants.

## 1. A warrior is never focused on fear.

Spiritual warfare requires absolute, supreme confidence in who God is and what He can do. The warrior's acknowledged weakness should get little attention compared with the strength and power of God. Admittedly, we all have weaknesses and "issues." But the quickest way to "wimp out" is to focus on our faults and our unworthiness—or the giant-sized strength of our opposition.

Often, representatives of the media interview me regarding my ministry, and they ask me, "Don't you ever get afraid? Haven't bad things happened to you in your work as an exorcist?" Yes, some bad things have happened to me, but no, I am not afraid. I have been kicked and spat upon. Once I had my ribs broken. I've been bruised and bloodied from time to time, and demons have threatened my life. But I'm still intact and still going after the devil on a daily basis.

I'm not putting on some kind of bravado. I'm genuinely unafraid. I see absolutely no reason to be afraid of the devil as long as I'm completely focused on Christ Jesus. It's like conquering a fear of heights by walking on the highest, scariest bridge you can find—which I have done, too, the Harbour Bridge in Sydney, Australia—you simply refuse to allow fear to take over.

## 2. A warrior is right with God.

The best place to get our hearts right with God is in the Church. Getting our hearts right with God includes overcoming sin and strongholds in our lives, including ancestral curses and other hidden time bombs. Only in the context of the Body of Christ can this happen to the fullest extent.

Warriors stay right with God by absorbing the teaching of the Word and letting it have its full effect in their hearts. This is how they keep the devil from attacking and exploiting their weaknesses. Spiritual warriors demonstrate their commitment to their Commander-in-Chief by being faithful to all things related to His army.

### 3. A warrior knows how to fight on any battlefield.

David learned how to fight where the sheep were grazing, and then he was willing to take on Goliath on the dusty plain. Later, he fought from caves and hiding places. He was familiar with psychological warfare too—remember his experiences with eluding Saul's murderous rages?

We need to realize that much of our spiritual warfare is psychological warfare. So many battles are fought in our minds, because the enemy of our souls can infiltrate our minds with lies and fears. We need to learn to fight on that battlefield before we can fight on any other turf.

At the same time, I'm not saying that a warrior should be out there fighting on *every* battlefield. The word *warrior* gets used in a figurative sense for all sorts of conflicts, from politics to the football field to the stock market. Those battles will rage on until the Lord comes again. Our war is against the unseen forces of hell that are bent on our destruction now and to eternity. The spiritual battle rages on too many fronts for one person to be able to count.

### 4. A warrior knows what he is fighting for.

A warrior also knows what he is fighting *against*. In spiritual warfare, other human beings are not the enemies; the unseen forces of evil are. That's why Paul wrote:

> We do not wrestle against flesh and blood, but against principalities, against powers, against the rulers of the darkness of this age, against spiritual hosts of wickedness in the heavenly places (Ephesians 6:12).

More contemporary translations make that even clearer:

> *For we are not fighting against flesh-and-blood enemies, but against evil rulers and authorities of the unseen world, against mighty powers in this dark world, and against evil spirits in the heavenly places* (Ephesians 6:12 NLT).

Many Christians think that the future of the United States rises and falls on who is in the White House. I believe that some political and moral battles are worth fighting with conventional rhetoric and the ballot box, but that can be a distraction from the real war, which is the war against the devil. The goal of the real war is to win the war for truth, righteousness, justice, and goodness to reign in your spheres of influence. You're fighting to hold the ground you've already won, and you're fighting for lost souls. You're not fighting for fame, wealth, power, or territory. You're not fighting for the polar bear or against greenhouse gasses, either. Your battlefield commander is not the loudest or best-funded voice on the airwaves or Internet. Your commanding officer is not being interviewed at all by the news media, but that does not mean that you cannot tell who you are fighting under.

### 5. A warrior knows that losing is not an option.

Although warriors know that they are not going to win every battle 100 percent, the outcome of the war of your soul was decided at the cross. Therefore, losing is not on your radar. You can go AWOL if you really want to, but if you remain in the battle for life, as true soldiers of God must do, you cannot and will not lose:

> *But in that coming day no weapon turned against you will succeed. You will silence every voice raised up to accuse you. These benefits are enjoyed by the servants of the LORD; their vindication will come from Me. I, the LORD, have spoken* (Isaiah 54:17 NLT).

You have no room for compromise or negotiation with this enemy. Your Commander doesn't, so you shouldn't, either. You are policing the victory that Jesus won with His own blood. The occupying enemy hasn't yet accepted the message that he must leave, but it is your job to persuade him—with force: *"From the days of John the Baptist until now the kingdom of heaven suffers violence, and the violent take it by force"* (Matt. 11:12).

You war on the winning side. You may be fighting against an insidious foe who, as soon as you have won a decisive victory, shifts his efforts to another front, but you must commit yourself to this war knowing that He who leads you into one battle after another is far greater than he who opposes you.

# Chapter 3

# Your Identity: Turning Obstacles Into Opportunities

*Life Lesson #3: Be an Overcomer, Not a Succumber*

I'M sure it seemed kind of dumb to the children of Israel, especially after several days of it. Joshua had told them to walk silently around the city carrying the ark of the covenant—while the people of Jericho probably laughed at them over the wall as if they were an army of nutcases.

To their credit, though, none of them broke rank. They plodded around the periphery of the city walls once a day for six days. None of them grumbled or retaliated. Nobody so much as spat in the direction the mockery was coming from. In the midst of the troops, seven priests trumpeted on their seven ram's horns, but the men of war were forbidden from uttering a single word.

God's angel had told Joshua exactly what to do, and it was not anything that he could have learned in a military academy. He was to lead the children of Israel around the outside of the city walls of Jericho once a day for six days and then make seven complete circles on the seventh day. (See Joshua 5:13-15; 6:1-5.) After seven circuits had been completed, Joshua would say to the people, *"Shout, for the Lord has given you the city!"* and the priests would accompany their deafening shouts with sustained blasts on their ram's horns. (See Joshua 6:16.)

For the first six days, the strategy was not making an obvious difference. The men would file back into their camp and wait for the dawning of the next day to march around the city again. Six times they did it. But the seventh day was different. Without succumbing to negative expectations or resorting to bribing their way into the city, the people of Israel proved on the seventh day that they would overcome.

On the seventh day, they marched as usual around the city, ram's horns blaring. But instead of stopping after one round, they kept going until they had completed seven turns around the outside of the citadel. Joshua gave the signal.

> *And the people shouted with a great shout, [and] the wall fell down flat. Then the people went up into the city, every man straight before him, and they took the city (Joshua 6:20 NIV).*

Overcomers—that's what they were. No doubt about it. The perseverance was worth it, along with the obedience. They did not become overcomers because of their superior fire power or because they had infiltrated the enemy ranks. It was not a matter of sheer strength or shrewdness. It was a matter of listening to God and doing what He told them to do, down to the last detail. Victory was assured—*if* they would claim it God's way.

## THE GREATEST OVERCOMER OF ALL

The Greek word *nikao* means one who prevails, conquers, and gets the victory over an insurmountable difficulty. In English translations of the Bible, *nikao* is translated as "overcome."[1] Jesus used the word when He declared to John:

> *To him who overcomes I will grant to sit with Me on My throne, as I also overcame and sat down with My Father on His throne (Revelation 3:21).*

The throne is the place of God's authority, where we shall reign with Him for eternity—if we have spent our earthly lives pressing forward in the strength that Jesus supplies so that we can qualify to become overcomers alongside Him.

Jesus Christ was the greatest overcomer of all time. He overcame the Destroyer and death itself. His victory makes it possible for us to overcome not only death, but also the devil's interference in our lives on this Earth. He said, *"...In the world you will have tribulation; but be of good cheer, I have overcome the world"* (John 16:33).

Whenever you feel like giving in to feelings of discouragement, hate, or apathy, remember that Jesus has paved the way out of any pit. You can overcome any problem with His powerful assistance. Just as He conquered sin and death, so you too, through the power of His Holy Spirit, will be changed from a person who succumbs to trials into someone who overcomes them. You will be strengthened to fight the good fight of faith.

The Bible tells us, *"Whatever is born of God overcomes the world. And this is the victory that has overcome the world—our faith"* (1 John 5:4). In order to start growing into a victorious overcomer, you must be born again. This might seem obvious—but then again, perhaps not, considering the large number of Christians who never recognize their destiny as overcomers.

Scripture asks, *"Do you not know that we shall judge angels? How much more, things that pertain to this life?"* (1 Cor. 6:3). Steadily, as we respond to the mentoring of the Holy Spirit and allow God to teach and mold us, we grow in both freedom and authority. Our goal is no less than His: to be granted the right to sit on the overcomer's throne.

Once in position on the throne of God's authority, we can expect to experience firsthand three realities. Each of them is mentioned in the same verse of the Revelation of John:

1. *"He who overcomes shall inherit all things..."* (Rev. 21:7).

2. *"...and I will be his God..."* (Rev. 21:7).

3. *"...and he shall be My son"* (Rev. 21:7).

We have been elevated to rule and reign with Him. We don't have to wait for Heaven. It begins now, right where we are.

## WHAT DOES AN OVERCOMER OVERCOME?

What does an overcomer overcome, anyway? Sin? Temptation? Satanic attack? Yes, and more. An overcomer overcomes every influence of the world, the flesh, and the devil—without compromising or resorting to legalistic means. Most of the time, this means hard labor, effort, struggle, actual warring. It never means achieving heavenly rest for more than short interludes while still on this Earth.

Paul was an overcomer, and if you stop and think about it, you realize how difficult his life became after he met the Lord Jesus on the road to Damascus. The Lord had told his rescuer Ananias, *"I will show him how many things he must suffer for My name's sake"* (Acts 9:16), and it came to pass. For most of his Christian life, Paul was attacked, oppressed, and threatened. Yet he didn't complain about it. He found that the rewards were well worth the struggles, *"as sorrowful, yet always rejoicing; as poor, yet making many rich; as having nothing, and yet possessing all things"* (2 Cor. 6:10).

Paul knew that Christians must be able to live with the perplexing quandaries of life. His outward circumstances would seem to have forced him to live most of his adult life as a defeated, dejected, and discouraged person (a "succumber"), but that was not true of him. Even when he was in prison and in pain, tortured with uncertainty and crushed by his feeling of responsibility for the people he pastored, he managed to remain an overcomer inwardly. This made him just like his Lord and Savior Jesus, whose death on the cross appeared to have been a resounding defeat until He rose again to deliver Himself and everyone who would name His name.

# YOU CAN BE A SUCCUMBER IF YOU WANT TO

While I realize that *succumber* is not an actual word, it does convey the sense of what I want you, the reader, to understand. One who *succumbs* surrenders, and thus a *succumber* (used as a noun) yields to defeat and despair, as opposed to an overcomer, who conquers and prevails over life's vicissitudes.

If you decide that this idea of being an overcomer sounds intimidating and you'd rather not risk your neck, you can take the "easy" way out. You can quit trying, stop asking the Holy Spirit for help, abandon your efforts to understand God's will and ways, and just succumb to the forces around you. You will never get commended at the throne, but perhaps you would rather have a less risky life on Earth. Jesus does not force anybody to come to Him. Even once we have come to Him, He does not compel us to follow. Each of us has free will, and He wants us to use it.

If you choose to be a succumber, you will give up under the weight of the pressures of life. A succumber yields, buckles under, gives in, and panders to insistent forces and pressures. Where do such pressures originate? With the prince of darkness himself, the one who exerts constant pressure against us because he is so desperate to derail God's plan.

A succumber succumbs to the pressure of the anti-God forces. A succumber allows him- or herself to be bulldozed. Still, as I said, you can be a succumber if you want to. In fact, if you want to be a highly successful succumber, I have some advice for you. Here (just a little tongue in cheek) are ten guaranteed steps to succeeding as a succumber:

1. Convince yourself that nobody cares about you.

2. Tell yourself that everybody is against you.

3. Act like doom and gloom is around every corner.

4. Believe that the successes of others are due to the lucky breaks they get.

5. Become convinced that your best efforts will not succeed anyway.

6. Presuppose that no matter what you do you will be misunderstood.

7. Presume you could do a lot better if others weren't always against you.

8. Constantly complain that your life has no real significance.

9. Always worry that nothing will ever work out right.

10. Be paranoid; surely others do not want you to overcome bad things.

## TEN DECLARATIONS OF AN OVERCOMER

I want to take each of those ten "succumber" statements and turn them around. Here are ten faith-building, Bible-based declarations that you can speak out. They will help you suppress your succumber tendencies and trust God to make you a full-fledged overcomer:

1. Nothing can separate me from the love of Jesus Christ. (See Romans 8:38-39.)

2. If God is for me, who can be against me? (See Romans 8:31.)

3. I choose to believe the best about everyone until proven otherwise. (See Romans 14:10.)

4. I will follow the Golden Rule and look out for the interests of others. (See Matthew 7:12; Luke 6:31.)

5. No matter what happens, God will never forsake me. (See Hebrews 13:5.)

6. I can do all things through Christ who strengthens me. (See Philippians 4:13.)

7. I will ask God for wisdom, and He will give it to me. (See James 1:5.)

8. I will remain steadfast, knowing that nothing I do for God is in vain. (See 1 Corinthians 15:58.)

9. I will do all things without complaining or murmuring. (See Philippians 2:14.)

10. I know that whatever I sow, that I will also reap. (See Galatians 6:7.)

## OVERCOMERS GUARD
## THEIR MINDS AND EMOTIONS

Satan wants to attack your mind, your thoughts, your feelings, and your emotions. He realizes that this is the easiest way to make inroads. The devil wants to corrupt your emotions, especially, because they can flip a negative coin in your soul. Emotions are more easily manipulated than cognitive thoughts are. Love becomes lust. Anger becomes vengeance. Fear becomes incapacitation. Sorrow becomes uncontrollable grief.

What started out as a simple, honest emotion, not evil at all, soon begets sin. I hope you know that your emotions are not evil in and of themselves. Every one of them can be used for good. God gave you your emotions, and He declared them good. All emotions? What about jealousy? That has got to be an exception. Well, God is known as a "jealous God," isn't He? (See Exodus 20:5; 34:14; Deuteronomy 4:24; 5:9; 6:15; Joshua 24:19.) What about fear? Perfect love is supposed to cast out fear, correct? (See First John 4:18.) Well, fear of God Himself is a very good thing, and fear helps keep you safe in dangerous situations. For example, when my family went on an African safari, our Land Rover was surrounded by lions and elephants. A healthy fear kept us safely inside the vehicle at all times.

While your emotions are not evil, what you channel them into may be. The devil wants to take a clean emotion such as fear and corrupt it. An overcomer sees it coming and refuses to cooperate. Like Jesus in the desert, a spiritual warrior can counter the lies of the enemy with the truth (see Matt. 4:1-11).

## OVERCOMERS TAKE RISKS

The 13th chapter of the Book of Numbers tells the story of the 12 spies, one to represent each tribe of Israel, who were chosen by Moses to go and spy out the Promised Land. Evidently, they were aware of the potential risks when they undertook the assignment, and they were gone for over a month. Upon their return, as you know, only Caleb and Joshua felt certain that the Israelites would be fully capable of overcoming the daunting odds and substantial obstacles. But they were outvoted by the other ten men. (See Numbers 13.)

When I look at the situation, I see ten men who were hearty enough to spy out the land for a month, but who became succumbers after their mission was complete. They succumbed to their fear of the strong and well-armed foes they had observed with their own eyes, and they succumbed to their fear of the unknown. Apart from this spying assignment, they had enjoyed a lifestyle of minimal commitment. They had grown accustomed to living in the wilderness, and it had treated them fairly well. All they had to do was to sit back and wait for more manna to fall from Heaven.

If they launched an offensive military action against the well-established residents of the land of Canaan, they would have to work hard. They would have to fight. They would have to shoulder responsibility. They would have to assume great risks.

"No, thanks," they declared. "Let's stay right where we are. Sure, the land is rich and tempting. Great blessings await whoever will fight for them. But count us out."

## OVERCOMERS FIND SOLUTIONS IN PROBLEMS, NOT PROBLEMS IN SOLUTIONS

The ten reluctant spies were the type who undermine every opportunity with a "yes, but." The obstacles loomed larger in their minds than the blessings, and they could see only the problems at hand. Milk and honey? Yes, *but* those people are giants....

They lost sight of the fact that God had already done the impossible in bringing them to the border of the land He had promised to give them. God had led them every single step of the journey, turning all of their problems inside out, drawing out the solution to every problem from the midst of the urgent need. Look what God had done in relation to their hard slavery in Egypt, the pursuit of the Egyptian army, their lack of water and food in the desert, and more.

With God's help, they had always overcome problems by finding a solution in the midst of the problems. Granted, their human tendency was to find problems in the solutions, for example, when they got tired of the God-provided manna and complained about it.

Overcomers can find a solution, whatever problem presents itself, while succumbers say "yes, but…" and miss their destiny.

## OVERCOMERS DEBUG THE BUG SYNDROME

The ten fearful spies reported,

> *The land through which we have gone as spies is a land that devours its inhabitants, and all the people whom we saw in it are men of great stature. There we saw the giants (the descendants of Anak came from the giants); and we were like **grasshoppers** in our own sight, and so we were in their sight* (Numbers 13:32-33).

Grasshoppers. In other words, if you think you are like a bug, you will be a bug. There's a proverb about that: *"For as* [a man] *thinks in his heart, so is he"* (Prov. 23:7). If you lack the confidence to believe that God wants to use you in His Kingdom, then you will never be used. If you consider yourself to be as insignificant and helpless as bugs, then bugs you will be, not only in your own sight, but also in the opinion of others (see Num. 13:33).

If you want to be an overcomer, you must debug the Bug Syndrome. Spell it out for yourself so you know what you're dealing with. In what way do you feel insufficient for the tasks before you? Have ever wondered why you were not promoted in your work for God's Kingdom? It could be because you come across to other people as helpless and faithless as a "grasshopper." You may have capitulated to your low confidence level. Your reluctance to take necessary risks may have relegated you to tending the home campfires.

## OVERCOMERS KNOW
## WHERE TO FIND THE ENEMY

Some Christians get it backward. They won't utter the name of the devil because they are afraid. They have become convinced that saying his name somehow conjures him up. How utterly ridiculous. I've had people tell me, "Oh, don't ever rebuke the devil, because bad things will always happen."

I tell them, "Bad things may well happen, but only if you *don't* rebuke the enemy. If you remain silent, he'll stay right where he is, making trouble."

Overcomers know where to find the enemy, and they stay alert. When they see evidence of his undercover operation, they speak up right away without worrying what other people might think.

If only we had had some soldiers like that at Pearl Harbor on December 7, 1941. The Japanese attack was not completely unexpected on that sunny Sunday afternoon, but only a minimal number of soldiers were on duty. Many of them were on leave, and most of the military offices were closed for the day. Although it was new technology at the time, radar was in place, and it was functioning well. The soldiers manning it detected some incoming planes, but they thought it must be a contingent coming from the mainland of the United States to Hawaii. An American destroyer spotted a Japanese submarine trying to sneak into the harbor, but after firing on it and reporting it, for some reason no further action was taken. Why was everybody afraid to talk about it? Were they afraid of raising a false alarm?

The enemy slipped in and calamity ensued, with torpedo attacks from the water and bombing raids from the air. Not only did the attack itself do great damage, but think of the subsequent declaration of war and tremendous loss of life that followed—all because too many soldiers and their commanders failed to take the warning signs seriously.

The same thing happens all the time in spiritual warfare. But overcomers who know who their enemy is and where to find him will not be caught unprepared. You don't need to be intimate with the enemy to know this information. You do, however, need to know a little bit about his habits. You need to know more than the fact that the devil exists.

I have made repeated trips to Hollywood to discuss potential television shows with various production studios. Before I went, I made the typical assumptions that Hollywood should really be called Hellywood because they market so much evil from there. And yet, I discovered something very interesting in my conversations. Instead of being confronted with demonically controlled, malicious people who were bent on destroying everything we hold sacred, I found only ordinary people who were confused. They had landed in Hollywood because they could make money there, and a lot of the reason for the money-making was directly tied to the kingdom of darkness. They understood that something malevolent was out there, but they really did not know how to define it.

They knew I was some kind of an expert in exorcism and deliverance from evil spirits, so some of them asked me to explain the very evils that they were attempting to portray in films. One day as I was walking out of a conference room after a meeting, a man pulled me aside. "Reverend," he said, "I am one of the top script writers in Hollywood for horror films. All I do all day long is churn out horror film scripts nonstop. I wish I could pick your brain. Because even though I'm constantly writing about evil, to be honest I don't really know what it is."

A true spiritual warrior knows what evil is, and he knows where the enemy may launch the next attack. He knows that the devil wants to attack from every angle when you least expect it. He can sense the presence of evil, and he does not hesitate to take preemptive action against the perpetrator of evil. An overcoming warrior has learned from actual combat. He has gained a spiritual sense of what the enemy is really like and what he really does. He does not remain on the sidelines.

You must personally discover who the enemy is and what he is likely to do next. To become a spiritual warrior who can overcome evil, you do not necessarily have to become an exorcist or a deliverance minister. Just as in any army, many people will be needed to perform support operations. But in your own way, you absolutely must get involved in the battle. Pay attention when I tell you: you do not want a "Pearl Harbor" on your hands just because you were off duty some pretty, sunny morning when the enemy chose to slip past your defenses.

I am not suggesting that you call everything demonic. Overcomers know what the devil and his demons really are. They will not designate every unresolved issue as being "from the devil." They do not look at somebody's inner inability to deal with life and automatically label the person demon-possessed.

Consequently, they will call it as they see it. If it really is demon possession, they won't assume it's harmless. They know better than to look for a wicked-looking little guy in a red suit with horns and a pitchfork and a forked tail. But they do not give the devil extra credit for human foibles and bad hair days.

## FIGHTING TO WIN

Spiritual warriors who are overcomers declare war all the time, but they do not waste their time declaring war against the wrong things. They refrain from declaring war on other Christians. They avoid fighting straw men. They don't see the point of blaming Hollywood or Washington, D.C., or the Republicans or the Democrats. They refuse to blame the devil for things he didn't do.

Unfortunately, a lot of Christians are like politicians. They are single-issue candidates. And just as single-issue politicians usually don't win elections, so single-issue Christians don't win spiritual battles.

There are too many fronts for a single-issue Christian. The enemy wears too many disguises. In order to fight to win, you need to be alert at all times. You need to stay in continual touch with your Commander-in-Chief. You expect to go to sleep with your weapon beside you, so you can fight at a moment's notice.

You cannot take time off. Once you have declared war against the enemy of our souls, you cannot ask for a timeout. Do not look for a halftime or a recess or a star break or a vacation. It's all war, all the time. Overcomers are warriors who, even when they need to regroup and step back from the front lines, do not let their guards down. They maintain a fighting spirit at all times. They're in this war to win it, not to wait it out.

Spiritual fighters never negotiate with the devil. This is war, not a negotiating table. Overcomers are not looking to reach a settlement. They are in the fight against the devil to achieve the all-out, total annihilation of everything satanic forces throw at them. They are not in the war to occupy, but to conquer. They know that Jesus, their supreme commanding officer, came from Heaven to destroy the works of the devil (see 1 John 3:8) and that they have been hand-selected to continue the combat. Why should they settle for anything less than victory?

As a spiritual warrior, you know when you are winning. How do you know? You know you're winning as long as you're not retreating, as long as you are staying right in the thick of the battle, come what may. After all, the only team that will score at all is the one that stays in the game until the end, without forfeiting. You cannot lose if you stay in this game. You may not be able to see the scoreboard, but, in fact, you're always winning if you're hanging onto the Lord, who is the mighty Victor. He already has won; you are just part of the clean-up effort. You're winning as long as you stay on His side, walking with Him. Don't walk off the field. Stay on the winning side against the forces of darkness by reading your Bible, praying, and staying true to the Lord.

## CAN AN OVERCOMER FAIL?

Jesus never failed, but the rest of us would-be overcomers certainly tend to.

If you have fallen short on a few occasions, do not become discouraged. *"For a righteous man may fall seven times and rise again…,"* Solomon wrote (Prov. 24:16). Failure is never final. Success, though, is never-ending. You can learn from your failures, and God's grace can redeem your mistakes. Repent if you need to, walking with increasing integrity and honesty, admitting your mistakes quickly and restoring what you may have fouled up if possible.

The Lord will help you treat failures as learning experiences. He will use them like fertilizer to help you grow. Some of your failures will become more valuable than your victories in that regard.

If you have succeeded, remember that you will have many more battles ahead. Never rest on your laurels. With the Lord's help, try to treat your successes and failures alike—as temporary experiences that can lead you closer to Him. Our great joy is to be molded into the image of our Lord Jesus Christ, the greatest overcomer of all. I want whatever it takes to achieve that, don't you?

Overcoming warriors sing a song of victory, no matter what happens. The reason David was summoned to play his harp and sing to soothe the tortured spirit of King Saul was because David was *"skillful in playing, a mighty man of valor, a man of war, prudent in speech, and a handsome person; and the LORD is with him"* (1 Sam. 16:18). His warring and his singing went together. When Saul's javelin sailed toward him, he was singing (see 1 Sam. 18:10-11). When the bear and the lion attacked his sheep, young David was singing. Like Paul and Silas in jail, the song in the heart of a warrior cannot be silenced. It's a song of victory and a song of gratitude to the greatest Victor of them all.

You, too, can sing the overcomer's song. You don't have to be a Pavarotti or an *American Idol* winner. Sing because you can do all things through Christ who strengthens you (see Phil. 4:13). Sing because you are more than a conqueror through Jesus Christ (see Rom. 8:37). Sing because greater is He who is in you than he who is in the world (see 1 John 4:4). Sing in the face of the fiery darts of the devil. Sing the Lord's praises. Sing about who He is. Let the song come up out of your heart. Your song lyrics are music to angels' ears, and they make the devil want to run away screaming. Sing a song of triumph to our God!

# ENDNOTE

1. See *Thayer's Greek Definitions* and *Smith's Bible Dictionary*. Greek lexicon entry for Nikao, The New Testament Greek Lexicon (Strong's number 3528), http://www.searchgodsword.org/lex/grk/view.cgi?number=3528.

# Chapter 4

# Your Character: Do You Have What It Takes?

*Life Lesson #4: Be a Leader, Not a Loser*

Satan does not want to draw attention to himself as he builds nuclear bombs in Iran, as he sentences thousands to die in Darfur, and as he ravages Africa with AIDS.

Satan would like to convince us that we really can sit down to talk with Hamas, that these people who want every Jew dead really somehow have a compassionate interest in the welfare of all people. He is constantly on the prowl, doing his dirty work without being noticed as the instigator of evil and often without being branded as malevolent. He is always lurking in the shadows of the heart of some ungodly world leader, prepared to plunge the world into Armageddon.

The devil's greatest strategy is to hope that we will completely ignore him. For a fact, he has convinced millions of "enlightened" people around the world that they can write him off as a fairy tale, a throwback to medieval ideas about ghosts and goblins. Meantime, these same people assume that natural human goodness should be able to prevail over horrific national crimes and ubiquitous wickedness.

The very last thing the enemy wants is to be caught in the light of God's Word, because the Bible reveals what his true agenda is all about. He prefers to keep people at each other's throats, opposing each other with harsh rhetoric and guns. He convinces whole nations that the answer to every problem lies in the ballot box or in whomever occupies the highest office of the land.

Let me assure you, if I were ever elected President of the United States, I would not be sitting down for friendly talks with the leaders of Fatah or the president of Iran until they renounced their genocidal aims upon God's people. I would not be communicating with rogue outlaw states or accepting their hospitality. The world could complain all they want. They could brand me as an unreasonable hard-liner. But I understand that world governments are under the thumb of evil principalities and powers and that no amount of negotiation will ever result in peace. Very real demonic forces control the thinking processes and the ideologies of masses of people all over the world, largely by possessing the governmental and academic leaders.

To bring the matter closer to home, we can limit our discussion to the ongoing moral and ideological conflicts that flare up every day in our own country. This culture war is all-encompassing and never-ending. It touches every area of life: families, friends, churches, neighborhoods, communities, places of employment. No part of our existence as a nation has been held exempt from the evil one's perverse influence.

Spiritual leaders wage war on behalf of their nation's soul. They are ready to fight the forces of evil anytime and anywhere, and they are not deceived by popular, secular arguments. A real spiritual warrior can see the devil at work within both the Democrat and Republican parties, with both the rich and the poor, with the whites and blacks, with everybody. A spiritual warrior knows that the devil is an equal opportunity antagonist. Satan lies to everybody.

The devil doesn't care about your income or your skin color or your political party as long as he can get you to murder the unborn or demean traditional marriage or tolerate the encroachment of crass and crude expressions of culture.

Nowhere are the devil's devices directed with more relentless cunning than within the Church. That's why people say that the safest place for him to hide out is in a church at 11:00 o'clock on a Sunday morning—because it's the last place anybody expects to find him. Where does he show up? He is in the gossip that splits churches, in the pride and ego trips that cause people to form factions, and in the denial of his existence by preachers who refuse to speak his name. He is in some of the classes and small groups that promote yoga or singles hooking up sexually. He's behind some of the "enlightened" views about alcohol and money that have made their way into the evangelical camp.

Your own experience may be limited to your own church, and you may not see any problems there, but take a little trip to other parts of your region or other cities, and you will find pastors who tell their people that the answer to their highly stressed lifestyles is to try to awaken their chakras through yoga postures. I have ministered to Christians who suffer from spiritual bondage, but who have been told that they don't need deliverance as much as they need a reiki massage. Most of us have heard the statistics about how little distinguishes the sexual mores of Christian youth from those of the secular community. I should not have to convince you further that we have a war going on. We have been called to fight in the culture wars of our country, and we have been called to fight within the Body of Christ to stop the intrusion of that which is demonic into the realm of the sacred and set-apart Kingdom of God.

We need to put a halt to complacent and compromised thinking and take the lead in spiritual warfare. Instead of saying "Oh, whatever," we need to strap on our spiritual armor and prepare for war in a corrupt society. "Oh, whatever" needs to change to "Satan, no! Not here in my family, my church, my neighborhood, my city, my culture, my country. You are not welcome here. I am stepping up. I am taking the lead. I am going to stand against you. Whenever I see you raise your ugly head, I'm going to take the sword of the Spirit and chop it off."

We must stop shrinking back like timid crime victims. If nothing else, take the lead in helping other people. Start praying for them. Start serving their needs. Soon you will notice that you are not so intimidated by your own personal challenges and that the enemy has less success in luring you into self-pity or self-protection.

Whether we're looking at world governments or local authorities, national culture or neighborhood life, global Christianity or your local church body, we need to make a difference by means of our prayers and our actions. In short, a spiritual warrior must be a spiritual leader, with a leader's grasp of the issues and dynamics of life.

## BIBLICAL LEADERSHIP

There are a *lot* of books out there on leadership, both Christian and secular, but the Bible is the finest leadership book ever published. The Bible not only gives us principles of leadership and guidelines for identifying true leaders, but numerous examples of leadership in action. Some of the characters in the stories demonstrate good leadership, even great leadership. Some of them show us leadership in action that is very, very poor. We can learn from both extremes, as we do our best to rise to the level of leadership that matches our destiny.

A good leader does not necessarily possess exceptional spiritual gifts. And yet the excellence of a leader's *character* will win many spiritual battles.

In the third chapter of First Timothy, we find Paul's list of qualities of commendable leadership. He's writing about how the church should determine which of their members should become deacons. Deacons were men who served the Body in practical ways, without whom the Body could not be strong enough to stand up to the challenges of being outposts of the Kingdom of God in a hostile environment. Their wives, if they were married, also needed to have irreproachable character, as did women who served as female deacons.

The core of the passage reads as follows:

*In the same way, deacons are to be worthy of respect, sincere, not indulging in much wine, and not pursuing dishonest gain. They must keep hold of the deep truths of the faith with a clear conscience. They must first be tested; and then if there is nothing against them, let them serve as deacons. In the same way, the women are to be worthy of respect, not malicious talkers but temperate and trustworthy in everything. A deacon must be faithful to his wife and must manage his children and his household well. Those who have served well gain an excellent standing and great assurance in their faith in Christ Jesus* (1 Timothy 3:8-13 NIV).

Do you see how the criteria for the selection of deacons mentions nothing about how talented or anointed these people should be, but rather focuses on their behavior and conduct over the long haul? The important things must be well-proven over time: how they treat others, how they conduct their daily affairs, how their families are turning out. It is much less important to see whether or not they can preach, teach, sing, exhort, inspire, or get people excited about something.

True spiritual leadership, in other words, is a lot more about your tenacity than it is about your talents. It's more about how you reflect the character traits of Jesus Christ than how you manifest His miracles. These standards for leadership in the Church have been given as a reference point for all believers in the Body.

Each Christian, whether a deacon or not, exercises a degree of leadership. Certainly each one of us needs to manage our households and take care of our families and others who are close to us. Wherever we find ourselves, all of us need to follow the example of Jesus' leadership as He cast out the kingdom of darkness and replaced it with the Kingdom of light, even if we lead lives that are modest and hidden and our influence appears to be minimal.

As Paul wrote to his young friend Timothy, the following personal characteristics are crucial for any potential leader:

1. *"Worthy of respect."* People will not follow someone they do not respect.

2. *"Sincere."* A sincere person does not speak evasively.

3. *"Not indulging in much wine."* This includes temperance in all things (personal habits, activities, finances, and more)

4. *"Not pursuing dishonest gain."* In other words, not greedy, a giver rather than a taker, a person of solid reputation.

5. *"Keep hold of deep truths."* Doctrinally levelheaded, biblically sound, not easily swayed.

6. *"Tested."* All of these traits have passed the test of time.

7. *"Manage his household."* People want to be led by someone who has been faithful to marriage vows, whose children are under control, and who has been diligent to provide for his family.

## LEADERSHIP IN THE BOOK OF ACTS

When we read the Book of Acts, we see the early church in action. They chose their first deacons by following a commonsense course of action:

> *Now in those days, when the number of the disciples was multiplying, there arose a complaint against the Hebrews by the Hellenists, because their widows were neglected in the daily distribution. Then the twelve summoned the multitude of the disciples and said, "It is not desirable that we should leave the*

*word of God and serve tables. Therefore, brethren, seek out from among you seven men of good reputation, full of the Holy Spirit and wisdom, whom we may appoint over this business; but we will give ourselves continually to prayer and to the ministry of the word"* (Acts 6:1-4).

These seven men had displayed common sense themselves, consistently over time. They had demonstrated already that they were filled with the Holy Spirit and led by the Spirit as they lived lives of commitment and selflessness. They were prudent and wise, but not in their own strength. Their faith kept them close to God and obedient to Him. They were highly spiritual men who demonstrated their worthiness by their godly example in everyday situations.

Their leadership abilities at first would be turned to waiting on tables, a menial task, but one that could not be completed without diligent attention. These men were capable of evaluating the needs of the church with competence, and they could execute plans with administrative skill and grace.

The apostles were looking for men of good reputation. Good reputations do not develop overnight. They are forged over many years of resisting temptation and proving faithfulness. These seven men had good reputations. Their honesty and trustworthiness had been established over time. They were emotionally and mentally stable. The apostles knew that they would be able to shoulder new responsibilities without shirking the ones they already had and without getting anxious or putting pressure on the people around them.

So the apostles laid their hands on them as a group, and they consecrated them to this new service. This was not a liturgical formality—the Church was too new for that. It was a solemn, but joyous setting-apart for ministry, both an endorsement and an impartation.

They took this anointing of leadership seriously. Soon, in addition to serving the widows, some of them had stepped into other roles. Notably, the deacon Stephen became a successful evangelist: *"Stephen, full of faith and power, did great wonders and signs among the people"* (Acts 6:8). Eventually, he became one of the first leaders in the Church to be martyred for his faith (see Acts 7).

Persecutions drove them far and wide. The deacon Philip took initiatives to spread the Gospel, and his preaching was very successful. Accompanied with signs and wonders, miracles of deliverance and healing occurred:

> *Philip went down to the city of Samaria and preached Christ to them. And the multitudes with one accord heeded the things spoken by Philip, hearing and seeing the miracles which he did. For unclean spirits, crying with a loud voice, came out of many who were possessed; and many who were paralyzed and lame were healed. And there was great joy in that city* (Acts 8:5-8).

These men were true leaders. When presented with challenges, they listened to the Holy Spirit and did whatever He told them to do. They were unafraid, committed, steadfast.

These character traits are all-important for any Christian to emulate and cultivate. They are the opposite of the ungodly characteristics that the devil would like to instill in us.

## LOSER LOT

At the beginning of the chapter, I wrote that the Bible provides numerous examples of leadership in action, some good, some poor, and that we can learn from both extremes. To draw lessons from a true loser, I like to point to the example of Abraham's nephew Lot. Don't emulate Lot! Instead, look at his life and do everything you can to avoid his mistakes.

We learn most of what we know about Lot and his family in Genesis 13 and 19. He was a wealthy man who traveled with Abram, and both of them had a large retinue of extended family and servants. The Bible tells us:

*Lot also, who went with Abram, had flocks and herds and tents.
Now the land was not able to support them, that they might dwell
together, for their possessions were so great that they could not
dwell together* (Genesis 13:5-6).

So they went their separate ways, and Abram, who was the older one,
allowed Lot to choose the best-looking land and the finest city, Sodom (see
Gen. 13:8-12).

From this we can see that Lot was convinced that the value of his life
depended upon his possessions and wealth. He could have become a vener-
ated patriarch, as Abraham did, starting out as he did on even financial foot-
ing with his uncle. But he saw that the plain of Jordan was well watered and
lush, *"like the garden of the* LORD," whereas Canaan was less hospitable (Gen.
13:10).

That was his first bad decision, and others followed. As it turned out,
his selfish effort to secure the best land for himself meant he had sacrificed a
chance to dwell with godly family members. Instead, he had chosen to make
his home with licentious, violent strangers. The environment of Sodom took
a further toll on him. You could almost say that "like attracts like" as Lot the
loser accommodated himself to the losers around him. He lost his spiritual
discernment and even his common sense.

When two angels of the Lord came to him, disguised as ordinary men, to
warn him to flee before God destroyed the evil city, Lot showed them Eastern
hospitality—even to the point of protecting them from a mob of city residents who wanted to molest them. The only trouble is how he chose to protect them—by offering his own two virgin daughters to them instead! (See
Genesis 19:8.)

The angels protected the daughters, and then they renewed their urgent
pleas to Lot that he gather up his entire family and flee. He complied, but
his sons-in-law laughed at him. Only his wife and two virgin daughters went
with him, and they all had to be pulled out of the house by the angels (see

Gen. 19:12-16). Even once they had escaped, Lot ill-advisedly bargained to be allowed to take refuge in the little city of Zoar, but that was not far enough away to keep his wife from disobeying the specific command of the angels not to look back. We all know what happened to her! (See Genesis 19:20-27.)

Alone in a cave with his two daughters, Lot had lost everything. At that point, he lost his last remaining shreds of respectability when his daughters decided to get him drunk and cause him to commit incest with them so that they might have children by their own father. (See Genesis 19:30-38.)

This is a portrait of an extreme loser! Meantime, back in Canaan, his uncle Abram met with angels as well, had his name changed to Abraham, and followed the Lord's commands to the best of his ability (with a few missteps, but which of us can claim perfection?). And he became the patriarch that we still admire today, one of the most successful and faith-filled leaders of all time.

## LEADERS ARE NOT QUITTERS

All day long, every day, you need to lead "raids" against the enemy camp. Never leave the job to someone else. Even when you are on a vacation, you cannot take a vacation from spiritual warfare. In fact, sometimes, that's when you need to fight more, depending on where your vacation plans take you.

At first, people think you have to be half-crazy to want to wage spiritual warfare day in and day out. But once you make it a lifestyle, you will see, as I have, the rewards of seeing people set free. Nothing is more wonderful than seeing broken lives put back together and injured lives healed.

Remember the words of Peter:

*Be alert and of sober mind. Your enemy the devil prowls around like a roaring lion looking for someone to devour. Resist him, standing firm in the faith, because you know that the family of believers throughout the world is undergoing the same kind of sufferings* (1 Peter 5:8-9 NIV).

Not only did Peter urge his listeners and readers to take the threat of the enemy seriously, he reminded them that *everybody* in the worldwide Body of Christ faces the same threat, day and night. Peter, one of the apostles of the early church, sent this letter off to be hand-delivered by Silas, who was another leader in the early church. It was sent to people who were suffering, from leaders who were suffering also. The recipients of the letter were in pain; they were frightened; they were uncertain about their future. And Peter wanted them to realize that they were part of a larger flock and that everybody was being subjected to the same challenges, worldwide.

The flock, under constant attack, must resist, Peter said. Using the spiritual weapons at their disposal and the ever-present power of God, they could survive any trial or tribulation the devil instigated against them, no matter how long it lasted. The same advice applies to us today. To *"resist him"* implies perseverance in the face of satanic onslaughts, and part of the perseverance comes from knowing that we do not resist alone.

Besides, continuing to stand firm in spiritual battle guarantees that the devil and his demons will flee. So your Christian life becomes a series of victories rather than a long string of defeats.

Caving in to fatigue or fear, however, guarantees that the enemy's attacks will intensify. He does not fight fair. He will kick you when you're down. And the sweet taste of victory will turn bitter in your mouth.

Which would you rather have: victory after victory or one defeat after another? Volunteer for active duty. Step up and take responsibility for the people and places around you. Lead out in confronting the devil. Do it yourself, even if others abandon you. You are still in good company, always. The mighty *"cloud of witnesses"* will cheer you on (Heb. 12:1).

When it comes to fighting the spiritual battle, you can't get religious and "leave it at the cross." You're *carrying* your cross, remember? It's one of your weapons, to be sure, but you can't shrug off the responsibility to confront the forces of evil whenever they cross your path. A good soldier considers every possibility of attack. Will it be by air? By sea? By land? Stay alert. You need to get so good at anticipating the enemy's next move that you can beat him to the punch and cut him off.

Peter tells us to "be sober" and "alert." Yes, the enemy has power and intelligence and malice. Satan has billions of demons at his command, too. Don't joke about him or mock him as if he were a comic-book character. But don't ignore him, either, and don't ever underestimate him. Be ready for him, by land or by sea. Keep your flesh and your mind under control and expect God's Spirit to assist you as you do battle—today, tomorrow, next week, next year, and for the rest of your blessed life on Earth.

In that short passage, Peter urges the members of the Church of Jesus Christ to get used to the idea that spiritual warfare will continue until death. Until the moment you go home to glory, you are going to be waging war. You are not going to get an honorable discharge until you breathe your last breath.

On that day, may you find that you have earned the praise of the Lord Himself. May He tell you, "*Well done, good and faithful servant; you have been faithful over a few things, I will make you ruler over many things. Enter into the joy of your lord*" (Matt. 25:23).

# Chapter 5

# Your Strength: Weakness Transformed

*Life Lesson #5: Be a Thriver, Not a Survivor*

The *TIME* magazine cover picture caught my eye—a giant-sized Prozac pill in Army-drab "camo" and the cover story blurb: "The Military's Secret Weapon. For the first time in history, thousands of U.S. troops are being given antidepressant drugs to deal with battlefield stress. Is that any way to fight a war?"[1]

As it turns out, the U.S. Army is using not only Prozac, but prescriptions for other antidepressants as well as sleeping pills to keep the troops on the battlefield:

> About 12% of combat troops in Iraq and 17% of those in Afghanistan are taking prescription antidepressants or sleeping pills to help them cope....The Army estimates that authorized drug use splits roughly fifty-fifty between troops taking antidepressants—largely the class of drugs that includes Prozac and Zoloft—and those taking prescription sleeping pills like Ambien.[2]

No one would question the fact that our troops function in very perilous situations and that it makes sense to use the latest survival tools to help maintain their ability to fight. But doesn't it seem like an extension of our society's attitude that we must take a pill for every ill and solve all of our problems with prescriptions?

The article made me think about how we in the Body of Christ may be doing the same thing. Are we, in a metaphorical sense, prescribing our own version of Prozac and Zoloft for the Christian troops who ought to be fighting in the spiritual war? Are we "popping pills" ourselves, so to speak? What would we call our drugs of choice?

One of the mostly widely used ones must be the drug of *denial*. Widespread denial makes zombies out of too many people in the Body of Christ. Here we are on a spiritual battlefield, and the soldiers are saying, "Who, me? I'm a Christian soldier, but you must be talking to somebody else. You want me to go fight a devil? Me?"

Our denial extends to the fact that we don't really believe the devil is active today. Try talking about spiritual warfare or demons with a group of ordinary Christians. When you bring up the subject, they'll look at you like you just stepped off the battleship *Galactica*. Although the newspaper headlines prove the reality of evil in our age, people won't face up to it. We have managed to explain it away. It's a fact: Christians don't like to use the "D" word.

Another "drug" we dispense to the soldiers in the Body of Christ is the drug of *instant expectation*. The message we preach gives people the idea that the power of God should hit you—*zap! bam! pow!*—in such a way that your problems will be solved instantly. Now, while it is true that sometimes we do feel His power, I don't care how much heat or electricity or tingly feeling you get in some experience with God, you will still have to get your feet back on the ground and pick up your weapons and fight the enemy.

Even if you get yourself into just the right place and the right time with the most anointed person on the planet, you should not expect to have your whole existence altered in a split second. A supernatural encounter will not solve all your problems. Most life problems are a complicated mixture of human sinfulness, circumstances, and demonic influence. We should not be giving the impression that God's power will give us an instant personality transplant.

I watched a healing evangelist minister to a man on the platform. The man said he had been diagnosed with bipolar disorder (manic depression), and it was pretty obvious from the way he walked onto the stage and expressed himself that he was suffering from severe mental illness. Yet the evangelist and his team were saying that if he could just get a jolt of the power of God it would fix everything. To make sure something happened, they cajoled, pushed, and shoved the poor guy. He ended up flat on his back, ostensibly in the midst of a supernatural experience that was going to transform him into a new person. When he got up, though, not much seemed to have changed.

The Holy Spirit is not an "instant fix" for the human condition. When people in profound mental distress come for ministry, you shouldn't sell them spiritual blue sky. You need to let them know that they will need some continuing professional help and that you may not be in a position to provide it. They need to know that even though they may truly experience God's supernatural power, including deliverance, they will have to walk out their healing. A broken mind takes time to heal. Mentally ill people do not need some kind of Christian alchemist to prescribe an instant cure. In the Middle Ages, alchemists kept searching for the magic formula that could change base metals into gold. Too often, we're doing a kind of spiritual alchemy.

I'm not saying that God cannot heal or that His power is insufficient. Not at all. His power is more than sufficient, and He can do whatever He wants, however He wants to do it. I'm saying that we actually limit Him when we boil everything down to human formulas. God's power cannot be reduced to a system or a procedure. Even when deliverance from evil spirits is introduced appropriately into the mix, all of our problems do not instantly vanish.

God does, however, want to help us. He does not want us to be left for dead on the spiritual battlefield. He wants us not only to survive spiritual warfare, but also to thrive in the battlefield environment. Without masking reality by pharmaceutical or magical means, He intends for us to flourish even as we keep fighting.

## SIMPLY SURVIVING—NOT GOOD ENOUGH

Jesus has created a bridge for you to walk over. You have a destiny to fulfill. He knows that to fulfill your destiny as a child of God you must *thrive*, not merely survive. As you engage the enemy in battle, God stands ready to heal your "battle wounds." It will take some spiritual warfare, often in the form of inner healing or deliverance, but every single person who wants restoration can have it.

I commend anybody who has survived physical mistreatment, sexual abuse, emotional deprivation, neglect and rejection, or satanic or cult abuse. Survivors are the people who continue to function despite adversity. I admire the determination of survivors to carry on in spite of impossible odds against them.

But surviving is not good enough. At some point, you have to take the courage that got you this far and walk past the wreckage of the past. You must quit focusing on the hurtful and unfair and even outrageous things that have happened to you and leave behind your victim mentality. You need to go to the point of the pain, seek out inner healing from God, and learn how to walk into restoration.

If you do not get free (and the sooner the better), you will find yourself under the thumb of the enemy more and more. He will have plenty of "dirt" on you. He will take advantage of your every emotion. You will feel like a magnet for trouble. You may realize that something is wrong, but you won't know what to do about it.

## RENEWED FOR A PURPOSE

In Chapter 1, we explored our God-given destiny and how to achieve it in spite of the devil's legal access to our lives and the many sin-filled strongholds that we allow to usurp God's Lordship. We came to see how step one of spiritual warfare is breaking free from the bondage that hampers us so greatly.

Since most people do not get free all at once (in fact, I don't think anybody does), we need to keep walking out our freedom. Your eternal salvation can be achieved in a moment of decision, but your salvation from the bondages of your past—and the past generations of your family—can take a long time. So just because you read Chapter 1 ("Your Destiny: Seizing the Reason You Are Here") and prayed the Declaration of a Spiritual Warrior does not mean that you will not need to revisit the subject anymore.

Life is like a road trip. Many routes can get you from where you are to where you want to end up. Your journey toward your Heaven-sent destiny began the day you were born. Whether you realize it or not, God has mapped out a plan for your life, and His plan for you is not merely to see you live "the good life," to prosper and be happy. As you grow and mature, you will discover more about your life-purpose and your destiny. Your life goals will become clearer.

Sad to say, our society has schooled us in self-sufficiency and self-reliance. God is somewhere off to the side. The people around us never think about asking Him for help. Although God is the author of our lives and the only One who knows how to help us thrive, we think we personally know more than He does! As a result, we find ourselves stymied and stalled. We can only see a few inches ahead of our feet as we journey along in the dark.

## START WITH A RENEWED MIND

If you want to know the *"good, acceptable, and perfect will of God"* for your life, you need a mind that has been renewed to match the mind of Christ. You need to be able to see things the way He does. You need His thoughts to infuse yours as He helps you see your relationships, your health, your finances, and everything else with new eyes.

The apostle Paul wrote to the Roman church, whose members were learning how to become established in the Gospel: *"Do not be conformed to this world, but be transformed by the renewing of your mind, that you may prove what is that good and acceptable and perfect will of God"* (Rom. 12:2).

He also wrote to the church in Philippi,

> *Finally, brethren, whatever things are true, whatever things are noble, whatever things are just, whatever things are pure, whatever things are lovely, whatever things are of good report, if there is any virtue and if there is anything praiseworthy—meditate on these things* (Philippians 4:8).

The underlying message is clear: Christians belong to God, and if they will let Him be in control, they will truly thrive.

## LEARNING FROM JOSHUA

Joshua had a destiny, and it was a major one. It took him more than 80 years to fulfill it. Having outlived most of his friends and family, he became the leader of the people of Israel upon the death of Moses, and God gave him some strong advice:

> *After the death of Moses the servant of the LORD, it came to pass that the LORD spoke to Joshua the son of Nun, Moses' assistant, saying: "Moses My servant is dead. Now therefore, arise, go over this Jordan, you and all this people, to the land which I am giving to them—the children of Israel. Every place that the sole of your foot will tread upon I have given you, as I said to Moses. From the wilderness and this Lebanon as far as the great river, the River Euphrates, all the land of the Hittites, and to the Great Sea toward the going down of the sun, shall be your territory. No man shall be able to stand before you all the days of your life; as I was with Moses, so I will be with you. I will not leave you nor forsake*

*you. Be strong and of good courage, for to this people you shall divide as an inheritance the land which I swore to their fathers to give them. Only be strong and very courageous, that you may observe to do according to all the law which Moses My servant commanded you; do not turn from it to the right hand or to the left, that you may prosper wherever you go. **This Book of the Law shall not depart from your mouth, but you shall meditate in it day and night,** that you may observe to do according to all that is written in it. For then you will make your way prosperous, and then you will have good success. Have I not commanded you? Be strong and of good courage; do not be afraid, nor be dismayed, for the Lord your God is with you wherever you go"* (Joshua 1:1-9).

Success was assured (and Joshua's destiny was within reach) only as long as the Book of the Law remained first and foremost. Joshua was supposed to meditate on it day and night.

The word *meditate* means "to dwell on in thought; to ponder; to bring before the mind's eye; to turn and roll over in the mind."[3] When you focus on God's Word to this degree, you position yourself to receive clear instruction from Him concerning His will for your life. In other words, you can determine God's purpose for you and receive His step-by-step guidance by means of daily reading, hearing, and confessing the truths and promises that you find in the Word of God. If you keep it before your eyes, in your ears, and on your tongue, you will align your thoughts and actions to His thoughts and actions.

Joshua did it. The best example, of course, is what happened at Jericho. His assignment was to conquer Canaan. His destiny was to lead the people of Israel straight into the Promised Land after their 40 years of wandering in the wilderness. Jericho was going to be a tough city to conquer. Joshua struggled. Wouldn't it be great to know in advance that victory was assured?

*And it came to pass, when Joshua was by Jericho, that he lifted his eyes and looked, and behold, a Man stood opposite him with His sword drawn in His hand. And Joshua went to Him and said to Him, "Are You for us or for our adversaries?" So He said, "No, but as Commander of the army of the LORD I have now come." And Joshua fell on his face to the earth and worshiped, and said to Him, "What does my Lord say to His servant?" Then the Commander of the LORD's army said to Joshua, "Take your sandal off your foot, for the place where you stand is holy." And Joshua did so* (Joshua 5:13-15).

Immediately afterward, God spoke to Joshua and gave him the winning strategy (see Josh. 6). Under his leadership, the people of Israel persevered, marching around the city for seven days before they could claim the victory.

In the same way, we too should persevere. After having immersed ourselves in the Word and after having submitted ourselves to the truth that God brings us (whether or not He stops us with a sword-bearing angel!), we must simply and doggedly persevere. Never mind that our "Jericho" walls still appear to be standing. Persevere.

Let's say your "Jericho" is clinical depression. That is a tough city to conquer. The walls are high and well fortified. Statistically speaking, did you know that the number of Americans on anti-depressant drugs is three times what it was less than ten years ago? (It makes you wonder if that many more people are depressed, or more of them are being diagnosed. But either way, a whole lot of people are very depressed.) We can't make a blanket statement and say that all depression is demonic, because it isn't. However, depression is the opposite of faith. In other words, you cannot walk in faith and be depressed at the same time. And as the Bible states, *"Without faith it is impossible to please Him* [God]..." (Heb. 11:6).

The Word also tells us that we do not wrestle against flesh and blood, but rather *"against principalities, against powers, against the rulers of the darkness of this age, against spiritual hosts of wickedness in the heavenly places"* (Eph. 6:12).

We need to wrestle, which is a very physical activity, in order to prevail. As in a real wrestling match, there are times of sizing things up, getting poised for action, even relaxing your hold for a moment. But you never, ever, give up as long as you have a word from God to hang onto.

When people are suffering from serious, clinical depression, their hormones and body chemistry change. They are unhealthy. Their bodies are reflecting a wounding in their minds, souls, and spirits. They are wrestling, all right, but they are not necessarily prevailing. Something inside is crying out for healing, and yet no one can achieve that healing by medicating the symptoms, although sometimes you may need to do that in the short term in order to survive.

You definitely can't achieve healing if you deny that you have a problem. You need to address the unresolved root issue, with God's power. You need to close the access door, the legal right of access that has allowed the enemy to wreak havoc inside you. And you need to dismantle the stronghold that he has built up with your unsuspecting assistance.

That stronghold is like an invisible citadel inside you. It not only walls something out; it walls something in. It is impenetrable, like the walls of Jericho—until you decide to get the help you need to win over it. I'm not a professional therapist or doctor or clinician, but time after time I have seen the stronghold of depression crumble like Jericho's ramparts. Stop thinking of depression as a condition that can only be treated with drugs and start seeing it as the symptom of a deeper root problem. Then, God will help you to identify that deeper root, and you can topple depression, one wall after another.

As you persevere, you will probe and dig until you uncover an actual traumatic event. Over and over again in ministry, we see that most depression, even a lot of biochemical depression, is behaviorally rooted in something unpleasant that has happened in the person's life that has been buried for a long time. When you get to the root, pulling it out will involve pain and tears, but it will be worth it.

By the power of the Holy Spirit, you will be destroying the dwelling place of the evil spirit of depression. Depression will not be happy about losing its former home. It will try to resurrect the walls, or at least make do with some of the old furniture. With the formerly strong walls in a tumbledown condition, actually like rubble, it will take a long time to rebuild, but perseverance pays off there, too. Put a sign up on the wreckage of your Jericho that says, "Under New Management." It took a long time to conquer the city, and it will take a long time to secure it under God's control, but you will have made a declaration.

Getting free is not like microwaving an instant dinner. Once in a while it happens miraculously and instantaneously, but honestly, most of the time, we need to wrestle down our foes and occupy the conquered territory with vigilance. We need to pay attention to God's instructions and directions. We need to discern His warnings. The enemy is still a roaring lion, even if he no longer roars at you from your fortress of depression. After you have pulled down your own fortifications, you will be positioned to help others pull down theirs, routing the devil from more of his strongholds and hiding places.

## BECOME A WOUNDED HEALER

Part of each person's destiny is to become a "wounded healer." That means turning your pain into gain, not only for yourself, but also for others. You can use what you've been through to help someone else. The lessons of your trials can become building blocks for your character, and you may be privileged to lead others along the same journey to freedom.

Now your authority over the enemy has changed from theory to fact. You have *won* a major battle. You not only survived the carnage, you found out how to be healed of your wounds. Now you can confidently lead others to the same healing. As you focus on where God is taking you rather than what He's brought you through, you make it possible for the Kingdom of God to expand a little bit more than before.

You do have to decide to act. After you accept the "prescription" that God gives you, you have to take it according to His instructions. As you learn to walk with a renewed mind and heart, you can expect to see great and unusual results, measureless blessings. The rewards are out of proportion to both the original damage and the amount of effort you contributed.

Here is a simple example of two men who chose to follow God all the way. Paul and Silas, you will remember, were thrown into a dungeon (see Acts 16). This wasn't the first time, and it wouldn't be the last. They could have decided to keep their heads down, licking their wounds, so as to not attract any further unwelcome attention. They could have taken matters into their own hands, attempting to notify friends in high places who could secure their release. They could have succumbed to self-pity—this never-ending cycle of abuse and persecution was taking its toll. But instead of choosing those options, they chose the option they had adopted as their "default"—they chose to worship, out loud and at length.

Their "crime," by the way, was that they had performed a deliverance, an exorcism. Here is what had occasioned their visit to the prison:

> Now it happened, as we went to prayer, that a certain slave girl possessed with a spirit of divination met us, who brought her masters much profit by fortune-telling. This girl followed Paul and us, and cried out, saying, "These men are the servants of the Most High God, who proclaim to us the way of salvation." And this she did for many days.
>
> But Paul, greatly annoyed, turned and said to the spirit, "I command you in the name of Jesus Christ to come out of her." And he came out that very hour. But when her masters saw that their hope of profit was gone, they seized Paul and Silas and dragged them into the marketplace to the authorities. And they brought them to the magistrates, and said, "These men, being Jews, exceedingly trouble our city; and they teach customs which

*are not lawful for us, being Romans, to receive or observe." Then the multitude rose up together against them; and the magistrates tore off their clothes and commanded them to be beaten with rods. And when they had laid many stripes on them, they threw them into prison, commanding the jailer to keep them securely. Having received such a charge, he put them into the inner prison and fastened their feet in the stocks* (Acts 16:16-24).

They had been victimized for setting someone free, and they had the bruises and bleeding wounds to prove it. They decided to ignore their throbbing body parts and their concerns for their well-being and simply praise God. Shackled, they were free in spirit already. The rest of the prisoners listened, mystified, but grateful for this pair that had been thrown into the dungeon with them. Suddenly, improbably, an earthquake rattled the foundations of the jail. The doors flew open and everyone's chains fell off. The jailer, who knew he would be held personally responsible for the prisoners' escape, was about to commit suicide. But Paul stopped him. Instead of witnessing a suicide, he presided at a new birth—not only of the jailer, but also of all of the members of his household. They were baptized before daybreak, all of them. (See Acts 16:25-34.)

## STRONG IN THE LORD AND IN THE POWER OF HIS MIGHT

You never know when you will have to be ready to engage in spiritual warfare. You need to fight every day of your life, but you won't always be fighting on the same front or with the same allies. Paul and Silas were ready for what happened to them in the prison because they had prepared beforehand. The way they lived their whole Christian life was both preparation and implementation for their effective spiritual warfare.

The sixth chapter of Paul's epistle to the Ephesians, his description of our spiritual armor, details six distinctive actions we must take against the devil, daily. The first one is easy to miss. *"Finally, my brethren, be strong in the Lord and in the power of His might"* (Eph. 6:10). Before we concern ourselves with weapons or strategies, we need to adopt a warrior's mindset. *"Be strong in the Lord,"* Paul says. He did not say, "be passive" or "be complacent" or "be prudent." Something tough and fierce and enduring needs to rise up inside you. It can't wait until you are in just the right mood, after three good worship songs and the pastor's prayer. It can't depend upon having had some recent successes on the battlefield. The advice itself is strongly worded: *"Be strong in the Lord."* No wimps allowed.

All Christians need to be strong in the Lord. We need to build and maintain our strength with some heavy weightlifting. Warfare is not for the faint of heart or mind. You cannot be a strong warrior if you watch pornography on the Internet or get drunk on Saturday night or surrender yourself to practicing yoga or some kind of non-Christian meditation. You cannot do spiritual warfare unless you are strong in the Lord and His mighty power. You can't even walk around wearing all that heavy armor without being strong, physically, mentally, and spiritually.

Why wear spiritual armor? Because we fight spiritual foes:

> *Put on the whole armor of God, that you may be able to stand against the wiles of the devil. For we do not wrestle against flesh and blood, but against principalities, against powers, against the rulers of the darkness of this age, against spiritual hosts of wickedness in the heavenly places. Therefore take up the whole armor of God, that you may be able to withstand in the evil day, and having done all, to stand* (Ephesians 6:11-13).

You have to reach out and take the armor in order to put it on. God will not just dump the armor onto you. You weren't born wearing it already. It didn't get engrafted onto you when you were born again. The armor of God does not automatically become part of your equipment just because you believe in Jesus and you've been filled with the Spirit. No matter how much you read your Bible and go to church, you will not thrive as a warrior unless you act.

You have to be intentional about warfare. In case you have not yet learned, the devil does not like Christians. When you stand against him, he will not silently slink away. He will fight you. In fact, sometimes all hell will break loose. If you really go nose-to-nose with the devil, he's going to throw everything at you including the kitchen sink—with all your dirty dishes in it. You need to be ready for him.

When he reminds you of how weak you are, you need to be strong in the strength that God supplies. Yes, you *are* weak. All by yourself, in your own strength, you are pathetic. Without God's strong armor, your battles will be over with in a hurry—and you will not survive more than a couple of them. So stand firm—in the strength that God supplies.

Satan will level every ugly accusation against you that he can think of. "I'm going to take you out." "I'm going to ruin your reputation." "I'm going to drive you around the bend." Along with the lies, he will send confusion into your mind. Don't be caught unawares. Get your helmet of salvation on (see Eph. 6:17). You need to make sure you have it on every day—before the devil starts to wear you down.

## ARMED AND DANGEROUS

When Paul wrote this letter, he was thinking of the armor and equipment of a Roman soldier. For a Roman soldier, the helmet was a sturdy cap made of thick leather or brass, and it had been created for that soldier. It fit him perfectly. The helmet guarded the soldier's head against blows from swords, clubs, battle-axes, knives, whatever weapon might swing his way. In your spiritual armor, the helmet of salvation is just that—your strong, individual identity in Jesus Christ. Confidence in your salvation and an ongoing relationship with Jesus keeps the helmet positioned where it should be—over your vulnerable thoughts and emotions. Keeping your mind centered on Him means that the discouraging and disparaging lies of the enemy will glance off without harming you. As you well know, a blow to the head can be fatal. Keep your helmet on at all times.

To protect the rest of your body, you need an assortment of armor. You need the belt of truth and the *"breastplate of righteousness"* (see Eph. 6:14). You need to protect your feet so you can walk, run, and stand on tough terrain (see Eph. 6:15). In one hand, you carry the shield of faith, and in the other, you wield the sword of the Spirit, which is the Word of God (see Eph. 6:16-17).

The belt of truth is a lot more than a skinny strip of leather. In the old days, the belt, or girdle, served as a man's pockets where he could carry portable items such as money. It was more of a waistband, and he could tuck his flowing garments into it when he needed to take action or fight. God's truth never changes. Jesus said, *"I am…the truth"* (John 14:6), and *"Jesus Christ is the same yesterday, today, and forever"* (Heb. 13:8). With the belt of truth buckled around you, the lies of the enemy can't distort the truth of God's Word in your life.

Like body armor, the breastplate of righteousness extends from your neck down to your thighs, with flexibility to allow for movement. Like the helmet, it protects the wearer from injurious or even fatal blows to the vital organs. Jesus Himself, who lives in your heart, is your righteousness. You clothe yourself in His righteousness; you put on Jesus Christ (see Rom. 13:14). *"For He made Him who knew no sin to be sin for us, that we might become the righteousness of God in Him"* (2 Cor. 5:21). The body armor of righteousness covers your heart so that your feelings don't have to be yanked this way and that. Wearing Jesus' righteousness, you can stand securely against whatever your enemy throws your way. You won't need to stand naked, in your own puny strength. You won't need to take a stand based on hallucinogenic visionary experiences. Your stance will be solid because He is.

What your righteousness in Christ can't defend you from, your shield of faith can. An ancient shield was not a flimsy thing. It measured about two feet wide and about four feet tall, either oblong or rectangular, and it was made of heavy wood covered with canvas or leather and soaked in water. Why did the Romans soak their shields in water? Because their opponents would often use flaming arrows. The Bible refers to the fiery darts of the enemy. The "darts" were full-sized arrows, tipped with fire. Flaming darts of doubt, discouragement, and despair will be launched at your faith.

If a flaming arrow strikes a water-soaked shield, it gets extinguished on the spot. If the soldier held it above his body, the arrows raining down from the sky would never penetrate. (That's why Paul wrote *above all,* in Ephesians 6:16. He didn't mean that the shield of faith was the most important part of your armor. He meant that you should hold it *above* yourself. The arrows will never come from below, but always from above.) So *above all,* take *the shield of faith with which you will be able to quench all the fiery darts of the wicked one.*

Remember, you do not stand on the battlefield alone. Your faith is not an individual endeavor. Just as the Roman soldiers fought as an army, so do you and the rest of the Body of Christ. History shows that a Roman contingent of soldiers would move forward by linking their shields together like a portable roof. If only the Body of Christ would march as one unit, we would have so many fewer casualties!

A soldier uses one hand to hold his shield high, which frees his dominant hand to hold his sharp sword at the ready. A Roman soldier's sword was a two-edged affair, anywhere from 6 to 22 inches in length. Used in close combat, it was the only offensive weapon the soldier carried. All the rest of his armor was meant for defense. A sword wasn't much of a defense compared to a shield, a helmet, a breastplate, and so on. But of course those items were not of much use to inflict actual damage on the enemy.

In the armament of God, the sword is the Word of God. As a spiritual warrior, you don't go into battle yelling "Confucius says…!" You don't find your offensive strategy in a fortune cookie. You get it from the pages of the Holy Bible. Jesus underlined for us the importance of parrying the devil's lies with selected Scriptures: *"It is written…"* (see Matt. 4; Mark 1; Luke 4). It doesn't take many words to thrust the sword into the enemy. One blow is all it takes, if you aim it right.

It should go without saying that you will not be able to stand firm for very long if you are barefoot. Battlefields are rocky and rough. Sooner or later, you are going to take a fall, and your feet are going to get lacerated if you do not protect them. Paul urges every warrior to put on the "shoes of the gospel of peace" (see Eph. 6:15). Again, he had Roman soldiers in mind. Their shoes may have looked like sandals, but they weren't like the flimsy flip-flops you see in a bin at Walmart. Their soles were made of thick leather, and they were studded with nails. Like the steel-studded tires that people used to put on their cars in snowy climates, their sandals were meant to provide traction. A soldier in battle needs the equivalent of four-wheel drive. He does not want to be driven backward, and he can't stand firm or advance without good traction.

The shoes of the peace of the Good News equip you to engage the enemy rather than fleeing from him (or falling before him). They keep you alive because they keep you on your feet, letting everybody know that Jesus is alive as you move forward. If you could not hold your ground, you would start compromising, and you would end up backpedaling. Eventually you would lose out with God.

## TAKE ACTION

Throughout this passage of Scripture, we can pick out the verbs of action: (1) "be strong," (2) "put on," (3) "stand firm," (4) "take," (5) "pray in the Spirit," and (6) "be alert." A spiritual warrior is ready for action:

> **Stand** your ground, **putting on** the belt of truth and the body armor of God's righteousness. For shoes, **put on** the peace that comes from the Good News so that you will be fully prepared (Ephesians 6:14-15 NLT).

*Above all,* **taking** *the shield of faith with which you will be able to quench all the fiery darts of the wicked one. And* **take** *the helmet of salvation, and the sword of the Spirit, which is the word of God* (Ephesians 6:16-17).

*And* **pray in the Spirit** *on all occasions with all kinds of prayers and requests. With this in mind,* **be alert** *and always* **keep on praying** *for all the Lord's people* (Ephesians 6:18 NIV).

In order to stand firmly and strongly, you need to take up your entire spiritual armory, and you also need to stay alert and pray. Get up on your tiptoes and keep your discerning eyes peeled for suspicious signs of enemy activity. Pray all the time, all kinds of prayers. Don't forget that one kind of prayer is rebuke. Rebuke the devil. (See James 4:7.)

In the entire passage from Ephesians 6, Paul tells us to "stand" four times. I have learned something about standing—literally. I've prayed deliverance prayers both standing and seated, and somehow standing works better. It's not just that the physical posture makes me feel stronger. I feel linked with the biblical soldiers of old when I stand up. They were not firing bullets from a bunker somewhere, dropping bombs from an airplane, or firing torpedoes from a submarine.

Like those warriors, we are not sitting down at a negotiating table with the enemy. We are not spiritual couch potatoes, watching the battle on television. We're not having a summit meeting with the devil or sitting cross-legged smoking a peace pipe together.

We are standing eyeball to eyeball with him, demanding nothing short of a full and complete surrender.

Like those ancient soldiers, we are not removed from the action. They grappled in hand-to-hand combat. They tried to cut each other down. Once you were down, no longer standing, you were out of commission. In those battles, as in ours, the last man standing wins.

Four times, Paul repeats it: Stand. Stand. Stand. Stand firm! You will do more than just survive; you'll thrive!

## ENDNOTES

1.   View cover for June 16, 2008 issue in *Time* magazine's online archive at http://www.time.com/time/covers/0,16641,20080616,00.html.

2.   Mark Thomson, "America's Medicated Army," *Time* magazine (Vol. 171, No. 24); accessed at http://www.time.com/time/nation/article/0,8599,1811858,00.html.

3.   As defined by Kevin Taylor in a sermon called "Discovering Your Destiny," accessed at SermonCentral.com, http://www.sermoncentral.com/sermons/discovering-your-destiny-kevin-taylor-sermon-on-knowing-gods-will-40493.asp.

# Chapter 6

# Your Voice: Making a Positive Difference

*Life Lesson #6: Be a Teacher, Not a Preacher*

When you do spiritual warfare, you're not standing in some ivory tower, pontificating to an enemy army. You're not teaching a safe little Sunday school class. You are standing in the middle of a combat zone, and it's a no-man's land until the warfare is over. The outcome depends on who's standing up spiritually at the end of the day. Will it be you, or the devil?

That does not mean, however, that part of your warfare might not involve preaching and teaching. You need to utter declarative prayers that tell the enemy his time is short. You need to quote the Word in every way possible. Paul charged the young man Timothy: *"Preach the word! Be ready in season and out of season. Convince, rebuke, exhort, with all longsuffering and teaching"* (2 Tim. 4:2).

The apostle Paul was both a preacher and a teacher:

> *...I was appointed a **preacher** and an apostle—I am speaking the truth in Christ and not lying—a **teacher** of the Gentiles in faith and truth* (1 Timothy 2:7).

Wherever he went—even when he was locked up in jail—he brought the Gospel of the Kingdom of God to the people around him. Paul knew that preaching was essential to bring people to faith in their Savior (see Rom. 10:14.) He modeled the value of God-inspired preaching.

Paul's preaching was accompanied by signs and wonders, including deliverance from evil spirits. Because of Jesus, his authority was unquestionable:

> God did extraordinary miracles through Paul, so that even handkerchiefs and aprons that had touched him were taken to the sick, and their illnesses were cured and the evil spirits left them. Some Jews who went around driving out evil spirits tried to invoke the name of the Lord Jesus over those who were demon-possessed. They would say, "In the name of the Jesus whom Paul preaches, I command you to come out." Seven sons of Sceva, a Jewish chief priest, were doing this. One day the evil spirit answered them, "Jesus I know, and Paul I know about, but who are you?" Then the man who had the evil spirit jumped on them and overpowered them all. He gave them such a beating that they ran out of the house naked and bleeding (Acts 19:11-16 NIV).

In spite of his growing fame, Paul never became a one-man show. He always made it part of his task to raise up others who could demonstrate the power of the Kingdom of God just as well as he could. He was realistic about the challenges of a lifestyle of spiritual warfare:

> This charge I commit to you, son Timothy, according to the prophecies previously made concerning you, that by them you may wage the good warfare, having faith and a good conscience, which some having rejected, concerning the faith have suffered shipwreck, of whom are Hymenaeus and Alexander, whom I delivered to Satan that they may learn not to blaspheme (1 Timothy 1:18-20).

Paul's courage and integrity provide us with much to study and emulate. Sadly, in the centuries since his time, many who call themselves preachers have failed to live up to his ideal.

## HOW DO PREACHERS GET A BAD RAP?

When people fill out surveys about the Church, over half have had a bad experience with a preacher. Some are genuinely traumatic, but for the most part the complaints fall into predictable categories:

1.  The preacher tried to control my life.

2.  The preacher wouldn't listen to me.

3.  The preacher wouldn't allow me to use my spiritual gifts.

4.  The preacher gave me bad advice for solving my problems.

5.  The preacher is only in it for the money and the fame.

On the other side of the coin, people don't respect preachers because they carry a false conception of what they are supposed to do...He preaches 20 minutes and solves all your problems. He condemns sin, but never hurts anyone's feelings. He works 14 hours a day and makes $200 a week. He lives in a modest home, drives a sensible car, has no need to send his kids to college, and gives half of his income back to the church. He is smart, but not more intellectual than the congregation. He is serious about his work, but he keeps smiling all the time. He knows every church member—and their kids—and remembers their birthdays and latest illnesses. He stays all day in his office studying and yet manages to meet every personal need of every member of his congregation on their own turf. He is young enough to attract the youth and old enough to engage the seniors.

On top of the false conceptions, people already know that words can be cheap. Therefore, they classify preachers with used car salesmen and politicians. They have seen too many high-profile preachers who "talked the talk, but didn't walk the walk," who have been caught publicly in scandals. The general public can undoubtedly name more bad preachers than good ones because of the proportion of publicity given to disgraced men of the cloth.

"They are hypocrites, that's what they are, dabbling in sins they keep telling others to avoid. They live in a fish bowl instead of fishing for men. They drive the sheep instead of leading them. They're pompous, way too impressed with themselves."

And anyway, what's so impressive about a guy in a nice suit standing in front of a bunch of people sitting in rows? Both in presentation and in content, the preacher's message fails to connect with the needs of the people who spend most of their time in a secularized culture. No matter how hard a church may strive to compete in this media-saturated age, the act of preaching ends up resembling a lecture dressed up as a pep rally. People find their smart phones more interesting.

For a fact, many pastors and preachers were never called by God in the first place. Some are just plain lazy, and they thought that the ministry might provide an easy way to improve their golf game. Others are constitutionally ill-suited for leadership and responsibility, and they haven't studied hard enough to be properly prepared. A large number have too many of their own problems, including problems with personal demonic strongholds, to presume to solve other people's problems.

## BOTH/AND, NOT EITHER/OR

Paul was proud to be a preacher. As I quoted above, he spoke of being ordained as a preacher, an apostle—and a teacher of the Gentiles in faith and truth. He "walked the walk" even as he preached and taught—sometimes teaching at such great length, evidently, that people fell asleep on him! (See Acts 20:7-10, the story of Eutychus.)

What made him a good teacher as well as a good preacher?

Interestingly, one of the primary characteristics of a good teacher is that of being a good learner. Good teachers never stop educating themselves. They know that the more they know about something, the more there is to know. Nobody can learn everything; there's always room for improvement. Paul scolded self-styled teachers, saying, "*You, therefore, who teach another, do you not teach yourself? You who preach that a man should not steal, do you steal?*" (Rom. 2:21). The very act of teaching models a lifestyle of learning to the people you want to teach. Teachers who grow continually in mental, emotional, and spiritual maturity will teach their students by their example, and, as Jesus pointed out, pupils tend to become like their teachers: "*...Everyone who is perfectly trained will be like his teacher*" (Luke 6:40).

Good teachers are good communicators. They may not have a perfect vocabulary or perfect diction, and their voices may not resonate, but they have learned how to present the truth in such a way that their listeners can identify their own mental, emotional, social, attitudinal, physical, or spiritual needs and find out how to connect with the power of God to get them met. Great teachers help their students search the Scriptures with clarity, transmitting truth through the many "filters" that people bring with them. Good teachers can really reach both the minds and hearts of their listeners.

Besides modeling a lifestyle of learning, as I mentioned above, good teachers model the very principles they teach and preach about. They themselves are "doers," not merely hearers (see James 1:22). They exemplify their own teaching. As much as possible, they give their students supervised opportunities to learn through real-life experiences. Especially when it comes to spiritual warfare and praying for deliverance from evil spirits, good teachers explain what to expect and then they send people out to "do what Jesus did."

Jesus Himself did this: "*And He called the twelve to Himself, and began to send them out two by two, and gave them power over unclean spirits*" (Mark 6:7).

*After these things the Lord appointed seventy others also, and sent them two by two before His face into every city and place where He Himself was about to go. Then He said to them, "The harvest truly is great, but the laborers are few; therefore pray the Lord of the harvest to send out laborers into His harvest. Go your way; behold, I send you out as lambs among wolves....Then the seventy returned with joy, saying, "Lord, even the demons are subject to us in Your name" (Luke 10:1-3,17).*

As I teach weekly seminars around the world (in more than 100 countries), I'm trying to equip as many people as possible to take their place as spiritual warriors in the army of God. In Eastern Europe, for example, we have trained entire denominations how to wage spiritual warfare. We have established more than 100 highly trained Do What Jesus Did/DWJD® inner healing and deliverance teams worldwide. My daily schedule includes many personal one-on-one Encounter and Intensive deliverance sessions that last from one hour to an entire day. My constant compulsion is to duplicate my calling in the lives of others. I strive to do what Jesus did so that others will do what I do and will teach others to do the same. In this way we *all* do what Jesus did.

This vision extends to our own family. My wife is often at my side combating evil spirits during exorcisms. When our oldest daughter was 12 years old, she performed an exorcism in front of 3,000 people in Africa. Our other two girls have stared down the devil on more than one occasion. They were able to do this because their father and mother showed them how and also because they have given their lives to the same Jesus who came to destroy the works of the devil on Earth. Just because they're not yet adults does not limit the Spirit of God within them. And no matter who you are, how young or old you are, if you can speak words of healing to the brokenhearted and have faith to look the devil in the eye, you too can set the captives free! You will move beyond mere "preaching" and pontificating to teaching others how to overcome every work of satan. When I say, "Be a teacher, not just a preacher," I mean don't just say it; do it, demonstrate it, live it.

## ABOVE ALL, BE A TEACHER

Whether you are a child or an adult, a natural-born teacher or someone who has been preaching since you were still in your crib, the important thing is to be a *doer* of the Word of God…a doer who does the right thing with the Word, that is.

For the sake of illustration, I want to give preachers a black hat right now and teachers a white one. (This is meant to show up the negatives in a memorable way, not to criticize preachers; after all, I am a preacher as well as a teacher, and I strive with God's help to be good at both.)

How can we paint the differences between preachers and teachers? Here are seven ways:

1. Preachers tell you what to do. Teachers show you how to do it.

2. Preachers hold high, unattainable standards. Teachers offer reasonable opportunities.

3. Preachers look down their noses at the weak. Teachers take the hands of the meek.

4. Preachers pontificate. Teachers illustrate.

5. Preachers demand, "Do as I say." Teachers implore, "Say as I do."

6. Preachers condemn failure. Teachers encourage correction.

7. Preachers stroll in cloistered cathedrals. Teachers walk in the paths of the people.

The world and the Church need more good teachers, not more pompous preachers. The ongoing spread of the full Gospel message depends on it.

## A DOER AS A WARRIOR

An active spiritual warrior proves to be a doer who takes action, the kind of person James was describing: *"He who looks into the perfect law of liberty and continues in it, and is not a forgetful hearer but a doer of the work, this one will be blessed in what he does"* (James 1:25). In the context of spiritual warfare, a doer is a spiritual warrior, standing ready on the battlefield, taking action.

In the previous chapter, we looked at the passage from Ephesians that describes the various components of the armor of a spiritual warrior. I failed to mention that the armor you wear for the Lord is not shiny bright and picture-perfect.

It may go without saying, but then again, maybe you never thought about it. Once you have wielded your sword against a foe, it will need some attention. It will need to be cleaned up and re-sharpened. Once you've worn your belt of truth, breastplate of righteousness, shoes of the gospel of peace, shield of faith, and helmet of salvation in a battle or two, they will start to show some battle scars. You will have a dent here and a scratch there. Some parts might be scorched with fire or punctured with some direct hits. You may see stains from the blood of combatants. After a little longer, the whole outfit will get tarnished by long use in trench warfare.

The important thing is not how it looks, but how it works. Does it still protect you, and can you still use that sword? Good, because that's all that counts. The Christians who parade around in burnished, new-looking armor don't know if it works or not because they have never tested it.

The problem with that beautiful, bright, shiny armor is that when the real attack comes, the wearer is not going to be battle-hardened enough to fight back effectively. Somebody needs to get their attention before that happens. Some teacher—who keeps his battle-worn armor on even while he's teaching—needs to inform those non-combatants that their peaceful interlude is about to come to an end (if it hasn't already). Sometime before the devil launches an assault on their church or family, on their finances, or whatever, they need to know how to fight back. When disease, dysfunction, pain, suffering, or disaster strike, they need to know how to stand strong and fight hard. It's up to the battle-wise spiritual warriors to help the raw recruits get up to speed.

One time, I sat down with a woman and her pastor husband and the leader of one of our Do What Jesus Did teams in their geographical area. She explained that she and her husband worked with the team, and that they had been using our training videos. She said, "I've been trained, but my life isn't working. In fact, just a couple of months ago I started to think again about killing myself, which I tried to do when I was a young adult."

As she proceeded to share the litany of horrible things she had gone through in her life, I listened for a while, and then I stopped her. "Ma'am," I said, "you may be a pastor's wife, and you may be doing spiritual warfare, but when somebody tells me they've had that many bad things happen to them, I know one thing: there is a curse somewhere in your family line."

Sure enough. Within the hour, we had figured it out, and she was completely delivered. Here was this sweet Christian lady, standing alongside her husband ministering healing and deliverance to people, the whole time carrying a 12-generation curse that went back to ancestors who had performed a blood sacrifice to the Egyptian sun god, Ra. This woman is not an isolated case. I constantly encounter sincere soldiers of the faith whose own personal lives are crumbling because an ancient evil was never discovered and eradicated. Some evil generational, family curse is still ongoing. Being a teacher of spiritual warfare does not exclude anyone from needing victory on their own personal battlefield of the soul.

## GET FREE AND STAY FREE

Even good soldiers can have issues. Each one of us has a choice.

You can take a pill of denial and say, "Well, this is messy. I'm just going to ignore it. I'm not going to deal with it. Who knows? It may go away." You can consult some preacher who will wham you and bam you and slam you and supposedly get you fixed in the blink of an eye. You can swallow the pill of extrasensory validation and shop around for an otherworldly experience that will block out the reality of your life.

Or you can buckle down and get serious. You can find a fellow warrior who really knows what to do, who will help you discern the root of the problem. Your freedom will be worth working for and waiting for. Look for someone who knows how to minister good, old-fashioned, devil-kicking deliverance if you want to banish the devil out of your life.

Then stand up, strap on your armor, and get back to work. Others are depending on you to be God's hands and heart to them. Because you have personally experienced the war and the victory, you will be more than a pretentious preacher, a dispenser of untested opinions; you will be a teacher with the wisdom of experience on your side.

# Chapter 7

# Your Strategy: Outgiving the Enemy

*Life Lesson #7: Be a Giver, Not a Taker*

I was alone in a Colorado cabin, working hard on the writing of the first edition of my book, *Larson's Book of World Religions and Alternative Spirituality*. It was a good day for holing up indoors writing; rain clouds covered the mountain, and the downpour was relentless.

Suddenly a sharp knock at the door startled me. I opened the door to see two rain-soaked and mud-covered Japanese-American girls on the doorstep. The car in which they had been passengers had just slid off the slick muddy road and had been totaled. They needed a ride to a nearby lodge so they could call a tow truck. No one had been injured, but they had left their friends with their wrecked vehicle and come to find help.

How could I say no? Putting aside all thoughts of losing valuable writing time, I ushered them into my car, muddy clothing and all. My car's upholstery was not the only casualty of the undertaking. As we drove through the storm, the fan for the heater stopped working and, as I fiddled with the knob, it fell off and rolled under the front seat. The car windows began to steam up seriously.

We reached the lodge safely, and they asked me for another favor. After they had placed the call for the tow truck, could I please drive them back up the road to wait with their friends? That took another half hour.

While in the car together, we chatted. In the course of the conversation, one of them asked me what I did for a living. Neither of them seemed to understand what a Christian pastor or Bible teacher could be, let alone what my personal faith in Jesus Christ had to do with real life.

"Where do you go to church?" I asked them.

"We don't. We're both Buddhists," they answered.

They were not too open to my strong assertion that Jesus was the only way to Heaven. As we reached the end of our drive and also our conversation, one of the girls summed it up: "Well, I guess we won't really know who's right until we're both dead," she said.

"But if I am correct about Jesus," I had to add, "it will be a little too late for you to find out."

Afterward, I thought about the incident. I could have argued that point on an intellectual or theological level. After all, I was engaged in writing a book about world religions. But from God's point of view, that would have been useless. Their minds were made up—for now. Yet in all likelihood, the willing assistance I had extended to them spoke volumes about the love of Jesus and planted a seed in their hearts.

Generosity—with resources such as time and energy as well as with money—is an often-neglected aspect of effective spiritual warfare. Lacking a generous heart, many a Christian has fallen prey to bondages of greed and selfishness. If I had not been willing to sacrifice my time (and the upholstery of my car) to the two girls on that rainy day years ago, neither one of them would have seen the Good News in action, possibly to this very day (although I pray that they have had other positive encounters with Christians and have by now given their lives to Jesus).

## A GIVER MENTALITY

People find it easy to agree with the desirability of charitable acts of mercy. But what happens when you try to extend that spirit of generosity to a discussion about money? Suddenly you ignite a controversy. It's as if the clamor of worthy causes has hardened our hearts and closed our fingers tightly on our pocketbooks. In self-defense, Christians say, "God does not need my money; He owns the cattle on a thousand hills. He made everything, and He owns it all."

But I say, "Stop focusing on the dollars alone. Instead, focus on the entire realm of *giving*." Giving time and talent and energy to God is on the same level as giving financial resources. It's the only way to produce fruit in the Kingdom of God:

> As the Scriptures say, "They share freely and give generously to the poor. Their good deeds will be remembered forever." For God is the one who provides seed for the farmer and then bread to eat. In the same way, He will provide and increase your resources and then produce a great harvest of generosity in you (2 Corinthians 9:9-10 NLT).

Your heart matters the most. How have you responded to your extraordinarily generous God, who has not only sent His Son to redeem you from destruction, but who provides for your earthly needs? Have you allowed His generosity with you to overflow into generosity with others? Sometimes a single big-hearted gesture does more to defeat the enemy than extended prayers of direct conflict. Your giving expresses the loving heart of your Father in Heaven.

What you do with your money is a telling expression, but only one expression, of a generous heart. When it comes to giving, your person is just as important as your pocketbook:

*I beseech you therefore, brethren, by the mercies of God, that you present your bodies a living sacrifice, holy, acceptable to God, which is your reasonable service* (Romans 12:1).

Each one of us has been given a chance to give back to God out of gratitude for His magnificent gifts to us. How will you do it? Will you give your time, your energy, your talents, your money? Will you keep on giving year in and year out? Are you a giver—or are you still more of a taker?

Givers are easy to spot. They share five characteristics:

1. Givers are motivated by sacrifice, not selfishness.

2. Givers give until it hurts, but they do not hurt after they give.

3. Givers let their gift go, without complaining about where it went.

4. Givers give out of the essence of who they are, not just out of their possessions.

5. Givers desire to give more; they do not wish they had given less.

Givers are always well supplied with more grace to keep on giving. They illustrate the scriptural principle for giving: You get what you give. Remember Jesus' familiar words:

*Give, and it will be given to you. They will pour into your lap a good measure—pressed down, shaken together, and running over. For by your standard of measure it will be measured to you in return* (Luke 6:38 NASB).

The apostle Paul, who received much in his lifetime, but who also gave even more, wrote,

> *He who sows sparingly will also reap sparingly, and he who sows bountifully will also reap bountifully. So let each one give as he purposes in his heart, not grudgingly or of necessity; for God loves a cheerful giver. And God is able to make all grace abound toward you, that you, always having all sufficiency in all things, may have an abundance for every good work* (2 Corinthians 9:6-8).

From what you hear from many pulpits and on most Christian radio and television shows, you would get the impression that the number-one priority of a Christian should be giving money. Not true. God wants *you* more than He wants your money. He wants you to focus on where you're called to serve first of all. Then He will show you where to give your money. If you gave to every good cause that came along, soon you would be in the red. There are thousands and thousands of good causes, but God wants your life before He wants your check.

Have you learned to stay close to Jesus and to lay down your life? Here is Jesus' own perspective:

> *I am the vine, you are the branches. He who abides in Me, and I in him, bears much fruit; for without Me you can do nothing. If anyone does not abide in Me, he is cast out as a branch and is withered; and they gather them and throw them into the fire, and they are burned. If you abide in Me, and My words abide in you, you will ask what you desire, and it shall be done for you. By this My Father is glorified, that you bear much fruit; so you will be My disciples. As the Father loved Me, I also have loved you; abide in My love…These things I have spoken to you, that My joy may remain in you, and that your joy may be full. This is My commandment, that you love one another as I have loved you.*

*Greater love has no one than this, than to lay down one's life for his friends* (John 15:5-9;11-13).

Often preachers tell us that if we give, we will receive, which can cause people to give with the idea of receiving. That won't work. If you give a certain amount because you are aiming for a certain reward, you might as well forget it. Your giving will be in vain. Give as God guides and enables you to give, and let Him decide how best to return the blessing to you.

When the members of the church at Philippi trusted Epaphroditus to carry much-needed funds to Paul, he thanked them and simply reminded them that God would freely provide for the wide variety of their own needs in the same way. *"All your need"* means much more than monetary repayment:

*Indeed I have all and abound. I am full, having received from Epaphroditus the things sent from you, a sweet-smelling aroma, an acceptable sacrifice, well pleasing to God. And my God shall supply all your need according to His riches in glory by Christ Jesus* (Philippians 4:18-19).

## DON'T BE A SCROOGE

Some people do not seem to have a giving bone in their bodies. They are takers, not givers, like bottomless pits that can never be filled. If you offer them two, they want three, and then they have the audacity to come back wanting four. No matter how many times you reach out to them with help, they insist that you somehow failed them by not going the extra mile.

Their insatiable quest for fulfilling their own desires includes very little inclination to repay a debt in measure or kind. No matter how much time you've given them, they never have time for you. When they're in need, they plead and cry out for instant intervention, but they never offer assistance to anyone else.

Takers are seriously self-centered. They may talk about God, but not because He is the center of their lives. They focus on what they wish God had done for them, not on what He can do. If you quote Scripture to them, they may brush it off as inconsequential, because it does not square with their personal experience. They talk about "I," "me," "mine," and their own problems with scant concern for you and your problems.

Often, they complain that the help they received was insufficient. The $100 you loaned them in a pinch should have been $200, and the advice you gave (and which they ignored) should have been different. Narcissistic, they see only their own interpretation of their lives.

## BE A LENDER, NOT A BORROWER

Aim to be a giver and a lender, not a taker and a borrower. When givers are not giving outright, they are lending. You won't find givers or lenders sponging off their friends and family.

Naturally we will find ourselves in need from time to time. It's not a sin to be in need and to adopt a receiving mode from time to time. In fact, learning to receive graciously and humbly may help us become better givers and lenders in the long run.

The principles for good lending are similar to those for good giving, and they apply not only to money, but also to your time and your talents. Good lenders have generous hearts and they have learned to invest wisely, save wisely, and spend wisely. They know how to control their money instead of allowing their money to control them. They realize that everything is a gift from God, and they also realize the importance of stewarding their money, time, and talents.

Good lenders know when to take a risk on someone; they can spot bad borrowers. A bad-risk borrower will never be able to pay back the lender, because he either hoards or overextends his resources. Whether we're talking about financial assistance, emotional support, or spiritual good will, the principles are the same.

The message is clear: be a good giver and a good lender. God knows your heart and your circumstances. He can help you become free of the bondages that contribute to selfishness, fearfulness, and immaturity. He rewards those who make Him the center of their affections:

> For God is not unjust. He will not forget how hard you have worked for Him and how you have shown your love to Him by caring for other believers, as you still do (Hebrews 6:10 NLT).

## IT'S TIME

Did you know that you can—and should—be generous with the devil too? In one important and specific way only, I believe we do need to give generously to the enemy.

What in the world am I talking about? *Give* to the enemy of our souls? Are we supposed to set up missions to hell?

I'm not talking about giving money or service to the devil. Not at all. I'm still talking about declaring war on him.

What I mean is this: It's time to *give it* to the devil and all his demons. It's time to not *take it* anymore.

It's time to pick up the sword of the Spirit and start slicing and dicing the devil. It's time to give him something to worry about. It's time to stand up, strap on your armor, and give him some grief, generously!

Every day, you can say, "I'm not going to take it anymore. I'm going to give it to the enemy! I'm going to give him something to remember. I'll keep striking him until he has been destroyed." We must be more vigorous than ever in our warfare. Every man, woman, and child who names the name of Jesus must fight. Our fighting needs to be more belligerent than ever.

Don't give up before you've started. Do not listen to the people who say spiritual warfare ended with the apostolic age. The devil is just as real today as he was 2,000 years ago. In fact, he's had 2,000 more years to perfect his battle plan. It's time to do something about it. Fight as if eternity depends on it. It's a matter of Heaven and hell.

I have made the point many times: spiritual warfare is not a quiet, healing time of soaking prayer. There is nothing wrong with quiet healing and soaking prayer as the *precursor* to real warfare, not as a *substitute* for engagement with the demonic.

Spiritual warfare is not worship, though worship may precede warfare. It is not fasting alone, though fasting may prepare the spiritual warrior for battle. It is not praise, though praise gets the heart ready for engaging evil spirits. None of these things by themselves—healing, prayer, worship, fasting, praise—constitutes warfare. They are aspects of warfare, but not an alternative to rolling up your spiritual sleeves and duking it out with the devil! And one of the best ways to land a knock-out punch to the devil is by *giving*, all that you have and all that you are. Takers enable the devil. Givers disable the forces of darkness.

War is not conducted by organizing committees and self-help groups. Spiritual warfare is, to put it bluntly, kicking devil butt. It's time to declare war on the real devil, not the people he has captured or the political and social systems they have set up. It's time to receive your marching orders, declare war on the enemy, and send him packing back to hell where he belongs. One of the best ways to do that is by the giving of tithes and offerings to the Kingdom and avoiding the curse of disobediences with your resources (see Mal. 3:8-10).

Get your armor adjusted. Get ready to give everything in spiritual warfare. Heavenly provisions will be your supply line. Expect joy and peace to fill your heart in the midst of this conflict, because you are abiding in the Victor, Jesus Christ. Give it your all!

# Chapter 8

# Your Exploits: Goals Straight Ahead

*Life Lesson #8: Be an Achiever, Not a Dreamer*

One of my pet peeves is Christians who come to church on Sunday, warm a seat, maybe contribute a little to the offering, smile on their way out—and feel as if they have just done their good Christian duty. They have missed their high calling in Christ Jesus, and they are likely to keep missing it unless something jars them out of their complacency.

Not many Christians have accepted their calling in Christ. They just go about being good Christians and good citizens in their communities, assuming that's the whole point. They are just putting in their time. They remain uncommitted to their calling because they do not even know they have a calling in the first place. They are saved, but they don't serve.

What do I mean by "calling"? Every single believer has one, and it's not just to occupy space and suck air. Your calling is the compulsion to do something with your purpose. Not to think about doing something, but to really achieve something. Not to be an idle dreamer who never gets his head out of the clouds or a spectator who watches life go by until it's too late to make a difference anymore, but to *participate*.

You find your calling in a number of ways. Maybe someday you're sitting in your room, reading the Word. Suddenly something jumps off the page, and you'll know—this is my calling. This is how I'm compelled to serve in the Body of Christ. Other people get one of those so-called "aha" moments when they receive an insight of direct revelation. You could be doing almost any-thing when the Holy Spirit speaks to your heart and shows you what you're supposed to do. More likely, it may "grow on you" gradually, as you serve in various capacities and discover what you were created for. You may discover your calling seemingly by trial and error, "blooming where you're planted" in the Body of Christ, trying this, trying that, serving here, serving there. Finally, you find a fit.

If you don't already know your calling, don't worry about it. You do not have to discover your calling today. But you do need to take the idea seriously. Your willingness to pursue your calling is more important than finding it. Seek the Lord about it. Ask Him to show you your calling, and don't give up until you know what it is. God will reveal it if you ask Him. "...He is a rewarder of those who diligently seek Him" (Heb. 11:6).

God will not force you into your calling. He will provide a door for you, but you will have to walk through it. Your calling was established before you were conceived. You have always had it, although you were largely unaware of it. You may never fulfill it, but God will not revoke it. "For the gifts and the calling of God are irrevocable" (Rom. 11:29).

You may miss your calling, but it is never going to leave you. In fact, you can't drive it away. No sin you can commit will change it. That should reas-sure you if you feel you have somehow disqualified yourself by your multiple failures in life. Your calling remains in place even though you may not feel worthy of it.

## SPIRITUAL WARFARE IS THE CALLING OF EVERY CHRISTIAN

Some callings concern a finite season only. Others encompass your entire lifetime. But spiritual warfare is the calling of every Christian, and every calling has something to do with it. That's why I spend so much time talking about each and every one of us being spiritual warriors. We don't have a choice about it.

Soldiers have differing assignments and specialties within their units, but they serve in the same military body. In the Body of Christ, all members automatically become warriors upon being saved, and, if they listen to God's word of direction, they will find their personal calling or assignment.

Granted, many Christians become casualties early on. They spend so much of their lives licking their wounds and picking up the pieces that most of their fighting energy goes into recovering. They can't do much fighting for the Kingdom because they're still fighting their way out of the mess they have gotten themselves into. Far from being conquering victors, they are defeated before they get started. They're struggling with their marriages, their finances, their children, their health, and their general oppression.

They may have figured out their calling, but they are not walking in their anointing. Your calling is your compulsion to serve, and your anointing is your power from God to perfect your calling. Just as everyone has a calling, so every believer has an anointing just waiting for him or her. Satan knows about it even if you do not, and he does his best to make you lose it. I have had evil spirits tell me that they knew from the moment somebody was conceived what that person's anointing was. From the womb, they perfected a plan to stop it and steal it.

Your anointing is like Esau's birthright (see Gen. 25:29-34). Your choice is to treasure your anointing or to squander it, and too often Christians squander their anointing simply because they're ignorant about it—and ignorant of the enemy's schemes. Instead of warring to lay hold of their anointing, they wallow in *"the lust of the flesh, the lust of the eyes, and the pride of life…"* (1 John 2:16). They stumble from one crisis to another, never suspecting that the enemy is behind so many of their struggles.

The devil never rests for a moment from his task of befouling your anointing, because he knows it gives you the power to fulfill your purpose in Christ and to complete your calling. He knows it is sacred—but only if a person treats it as such by walking in it and using it. The anointing becomes a sign of your consecration. The degree of your consecration and dedication will determine the power of your anointing.

In other words, you can make the difference. Your diligent pursuit of your calling and anointing will enable you to walk out your commitment to Jesus Christ with faithfulness. The closer you walk with the Lord in your heart, the greater your anointing will be and the more effective your actions. You will begin to walk in your calling—and your spiritual warfare will pay off with a powerful, fulfilling life.

## RESIGN FROM THE SPECTATOR SOCIETY

The United States has become a land of professional spectators. Daily, Americans gain pleasure from watching others live out their lives—and I don't mean only on reality television. We're obsessed with people whom we don't even know. We prefer to ogle at what others do, even good and admirable things, rather than doing something ourselves.

We watch sports rather than playing sports. We watch news rather than making it. We watch YouTube and webcams, becoming voyeurs who are disconnected from the reality of our own lives. While we sit on the sidelines of life wasting the minutes and hours, the people we are watching are reaching their goals and sometimes their destinies. Like invalids who are bedridden, we seem to suffer from a deadly disease that conforms us to the world and keeps us from acting out the mighty works of God.

When people say, "I prefer to be a spectator," they mean that they consider it more prudent to stay on the sidelines, as in, "I'd rather not drive in a NASCAR race; I prefer to be a spectator." They want to avoid conflict or injury, expense or hassle. This ends up being the approach that most people take to spiritual warfare and deliverance. They don't want to get involved in something that appears to be challenging and that could prove to be costly.

Staying on the sidelines, however, does nothing to provide a positive sense of fulfilling a calling or a duty. It accomplishes nothing. How much better is it to become a participant in whatever spiritual endeavor God sends our way?

## BE AN ACHIEVER, NOT A DREAMER

Many spectators harbor dreams of greatness. As they sit in front of the TELEVISION watching the winning touchdown in the football game, they imagine what it would feel like to be that quarterback. As they play the latest video game, they visualize themselves as indestructible and undefeatable superheroes. As the piano student practices his lessons, he pictures himself as the next Wolfgang Amadeus Mozart.

Such a dreamer conceives of himself or herself as an accomplished achiever in spite of never leaving the living room. Dreamers live in a world of fantasy and imagination, seldom executing their impractical projects and ideas.

Dreamers and spectators boast of big ideas, but they produce few measurable results. Talking in the abstract rather than the concrete, their professed expectations far exceed their ability to perform. They tend to overestimate their capabilities and blame other people or circumstances for their failures. It's always the next opportunity that will be the "really big one" that pays off; they operate out of a gamblers' mindset. They find reasonable-sounding excuses for shirking responsibility, allowing their hesitation to neutralize their effectiveness. If they can find someone else to take the risks for them, they will defer getting involved themselves. They are the last to volunteer and the first to take a pass when a situation becomes challenging. Avoiding pain is more important than achieving gain. In fact, to them the glass can be "half empty" much of the time, as they see the giants in the land instead of the milk and honey.

Some dreamers are quite persuasive, especially those who profess to hear from God. I have known a lot of people who have spouted forth big ideas about what they were going to do for God, only to watch them be disqualified by the inconsistencies of their Christian walk and the lack of fruit in their lives. The Bible refers to such people:

> If there arises among you a prophet or a dreamer of dreams, and he gives you a sign or a wonder, and the sign or the wonder comes to pass, of which he spoke to you, saying, "Let us go after other gods"—which you have not known—"and let us serve them," you shall not listen to the words of that prophet or that dreamer of dreams, for the LORD your God is testing you to know whether you love the LORD your God with all your heart and with all your soul (Deuteronomy 13:1-3).

In contrast, a true achiever will be someone who has embraced his or her calling and anointing and who has pursued God's desires. This is the person who can properly and successfully carry out the achievement of a definite goal. It starts with standing up and volunteering for active duty.

An achiever is willing to take more than a few risks and can handle public criticism without losing his or her self-esteem. Like Peter, achievers are willing to get out of the boat and at least attempt to walk on water (see Matt. 14:25-31). Their egos are not at stake. They do not equate a temporary defeat with a permanent character flaw. They can keep achieving great things for God even when they are hidden from adulation or from the notice of other people. They are performing for the "audience of One"—the Lord Himself. As they test their strengths in the crucible of real conflict, they discover their limitations, and they learn from this discovery. They never expect to win every single time, but they fully believe that having some wins with losses is better than never having ventured forth onto the battlefield in the first place.

Learning from their experiences, they methodically build upon their past successes, one at a time. They never promise more than they can produce; they are reasonable about their expectations; and they do not pridefully overreach. In spiritual warfare, as in all other aspects of life, achievers give credit to others who have helped them along the way. They realize that God is the one who has given them their gifts and talents and that He has opened the doors before them.

Dreams are the stuff from which great ideas are forged. Watching the world go by and dreaming of personal achievement are good beginnings. But to be fulfilled, dreams require action, implementation, and hard work. Lasting achievements are always built on a solid foundation of tried and tested theories, ideas which have proven to be durable and down-to-earth, even when they originate in Heaven.

## GOING BEYOND THE END OF YOUR DREAM

As a spiritual dreamer who makes a real difference in the world, you can be encouraged by the seeming failure of Walt Disney, who wanted to build a utopian "city of the future" in Florida on land that was useless for agriculture. He tried. He poured money into the development of "Epcot," an acronym for Experimental Prototype Community of Tomorrow. He quietly acquired about 25,000 acres of the swampy land, but failed to persuade the local authorities to issue the necessary permits. The holdup was this: the authorities wanted him to develop a theme park first, bigger and better than Disneyland in Southern California.

He reoriented to build the park first. Marketed as "Disney World," its name on official documents was the Reedy Creek Improvement District. Before Disney could turn his attention back to the development of his dream community, he died. The Disney corporation did not share his dream, so they concentrated all of their attention on the "Magic Kingdom," which is now a worldwide magnet for tourism from families who want clean entertainment.

What happened to the town of Epcot? An article in *National Geographic* explains:

> People thronged to the Magic Kingdom to see with their own
> eyes what they'd seen on TELEVISION, but Epcot, Disney's

cherished project of creating a futuristic community where people lived and worked in high-tech harmony, never became a reality. People weren't interested in Disney's edgeless version of tomorrow. Epcot was such a failure that Disney officials faced the embarrassing prospect of shutting it down. Instead, they turned it into another tourist attraction. Today Epcot offers a nostalgic pastiche of a 1940s seashore vacation.[1]

My point is a simple one: You can still achieve great things even if you meet with roadblocks on the way. And believe me, you will meet roadblocks. Jesus did. Paul did. You will not always end up with what you thought you were aiming for. But if you make the effort to try, you end up with something that God can bless.

## BLESSING FOLLOWS OBEDIENCE

A man or woman of God will refuse to be sidelined by setbacks. Instead, they will see difficulties as launching pads for the next achievement for God.

Success or failure in the Christian life hinges upon whether or not we believe God enough to test His promises. The whole Bible is about what God will do if we will step up onto the stage of life and act out what He has declared in His Word. God doesn't want to see us performing for a temporary endorsement like an Emmy or a Grammy or an Oscar. He doesn't want us to strive for the cheers of adulation or the spotlight. Instead, He wants us to put on our spiritual armor, shoulder our crosses, and fight to receive the benefits of obedience to His voice:

> If you fully obey the LORD your God and carefully follow all His commands I give you today, the LORD your God will set you high above all the nations on earth. All these blessings will come upon you and accompany you if you obey the LORD your God: You will be blessed in the city and blessed in the country. The

*fruit of your womb will be blessed, and the crops of your land and the young of your livestock—the calves of your herds and the lambs of your flocks. Your basket and your kneading trough will be blessed. You will be blessed when you come in and blessed when you go out. The LORD will grant that the enemies who rise up against you will be defeated before you. They will come at you from one direction but flee from you in seven. The LORD will send a blessing on your barns and on everything you put your hand to. The LORD your God will bless you in the land He is giving you. The LORD will establish you as His holy people, as He promised you on oath, if you keep the commands of the LORD your God and walk in obedience to Him. Then all the peoples on earth will see that you are called by the name of the LORD, and they will fear you. The LORD will grant you abundant prosperity—in the fruit of your womb, the young of your livestock and the crops of your ground—in the land He swore to your ancestors to give you.*

*The LORD will open the heavens, the storehouse of His bounty, to send rain on your land in season and to bless all the work of your hands. You will lend to many nations but will borrow from none. The LORD will make you the head, not the tail. If you pay attention to the commands of the LORD your God that I give you this day and carefully follow them, you will always be at the top, never at the bottom. Do not turn aside from any of the commands I give you today, to the right or to the left, following other gods and serving them* (Deuteronomy 28:1-14 NIV).

If you faithfully obey the voice of your Commander, you will have success on any battlefield. Your heavenly rewards will accompany you wherever you go, and they will not be contingent upon your circumstances. Blessings will accrue both to your possessions and your progeny, both to what you own and what you claim as your family bloodline. You will be blessed in *who you are*, regardless of where you are. Your enemies will be defeated supernaturally, as divine favor follows you through your abundant life. You will call the shots, rather than having shots find their mark in you. Your multi-faceted prosperity will exceed your expectations, allowing you to share with others.

Your blessings will come at a price, to be sure:

> *"Truly I tell you," Jesus replied, "no one who has left home or brothers or sisters or mother or father or children or fields for me and the gospel will fail to receive a hundred times as much in this present age: homes, brothers, sisters, mothers, children and fields—along with persecutions—and in the age to come eternal life"* (Mark 10:29-30 NIV).

God wants us to out-perform His Son:

> *Very truly I tell you, whoever believes in Me will do the works I have been doing, and they will do even greater things than these, because I am going to the Father* (John 14:12 NIV).

Dreaming isn't enough. It may lead to great achievements, but dreaming can also be a way of avoidance. True achievers understand their…

- *Purpose*—the reason God put them on Earth.

- *Calling*—the implementation of their purpose.

- *Anointing*—the power to perform their purpose.

- *Destiny*—the substantive, final fulfillment of their purpose.

Which will you be—a dreamer who fantasizes about spiritual warfare, or an achiever who wins real victories against the powers of evil?

# ENDNOTE

1.  T.D. Allman, "Beyond Disney," *National Geographic*, March 2007; accessed at http://ngm.nationalgeographic.com/2007/03/orlando/allman-text.html.

# Chapter 9

# Your Heart: Bonded With Others

*Life Lesson #9: Be a Friend, Not a Phony*

More than 20 years ago, I faced a long "dark night of the soul." I had one friend who determined that he would not allow me to succumb to discouragement or abandon my hope in God or my calling. He phoned me every single day, long distance, at his own expense, for several years. He listened to me. He advised me. He encouraged me. I will be immeasurably grateful to him as long as I live.

As I look back, I have had many friends, but almost none like that one. Not one of my childhood friends knows me anymore. After high school commencement and college, we all went our separate ways. In early adulthood, I thought of many people as my friends, and yet none of them has any significance in my life today.

Some friendships are significant for only a season. I have had friends who opened doors for me—or who forced me to walk through open doors. (I'm thinking of the man who forced me to do my first public deliverance.) One friend made it possible for me to begin to publish books. A couple of fellow pastors defended me and my calling in the face of fierce opposition from their own congregations, and one of them did not even completely approve of my calling. They were my friends, and they believed in me.

A friend attaches himself or herself to you by affection and esteem. A friend, without compulsion, necessity, or self-aggrandizement, promotes you as a person. On your personal spiritual battlefield, you always need friends. You will not be able to make it without them.

## NOT JUST ME AND JESUS

As I have been saying throughout this book, you must accept the fact that you have been conscripted into the army of God on Earth, and you can never opt out of spiritual warfare. In terms of friendship, that's just the point—we are talking about an *army*, not just "me and Jesus." None of us is a Lone Ranger, or even a Lone Ranger with a devoted buddy named Tonto. We can never stand on the battlefield by ourselves. Spiritual warfare will go much better for us if we have not only a loyal spouse or best friend, but we stand shoulder to shoulder with many others.

Although each and every one of us needs to make a personal decision to take an active part in the spiritual battle, absolutely no one can prevail alone in spiritual warfare. On the battlefield, you need the strong arms, the alert eyes, and the attentive concern for your welfare that your fellow soldiers can supply. You need wisdom, love, and words of encouragement from more than one other person. Other people need what you have to offer, as well.

Several Hebrew and Greek words have been translated as "friend" in the Bible. The Hebrew word *raáh*, pronounced "ray-ah,"[1] means an associate with whom we have a reciprocal relationship. It is used in many passages of the Old Testament, including Proverbs 18:24: "*One who has unreliable friends soon comes to ruin, but there is a friend who sticks closer than a brother*" (NIV). The Greek word *philos* conveys endearment and close comradeship.[2] The apostle John, who was one of Jesus' closest companions himself, uses the word *philos* over and over in his Gospel. Consider these familiar passages:

> He who has the bride is the bridegroom; but the **friend** of the bridegroom, who stands and hears him, rejoices greatly because of the bridegroom's voice... (John 3:29).

*…He said to them, "Our **friend** Lazarus sleeps, but I go that I may wake him up"* (John 11:11).

*The Scripture was fulfilled which says, "Abraham believed God, and it was accounted to him for righteousness." And he was called the **friend** of God* (James 2:23).

In the Bible, a friend loves dearly and expects nothing in return. If you stop and think about it, you realize that the truest friendship is only possible for those in whose spirits the Holy Spirit, the truest Love of all, dwells.

## JESUS' FRIENDS

Jesus said, *"You are My friends if you do whatever I command you"* (John 15:14). At the same time, He took the initiative to befriend people who did not yet obey Him in the least. Some of them became His disciples.

For example, Peter followed Jesus and declared his undying devotion, only to deny Him before the crucifixion. He ran out of Pilate's judgment hall weeping profusely because he knew that he had betrayed his dearest friend in the moment of His direst need. In response, did Jesus deny Peter? No, as proved by the touching scene on the shores of the Sea of Galilee after Jesus' resurrection:

*So when they had eaten breakfast, Jesus said to Simon Peter, "Simon, son of Jonah, do you love Me more than these?" He said to Him, "Yes, Lord; You know that I love You." He said to him, "Feed My lambs." He said to him again a second time, "Simon, son of Jonah, do you love Me?" He said to Him, "Yes, Lord; You know that I love You." He said to him, "Tend My sheep." He said to him the third time, "Simon, son of Jonah, do you love Me?" Peter was grieved because He said to him the third time, "Do you love Me?" And he said to Him, "Lord, You know all things; You know that I love You." Jesus said to him, "Feed My sheep"* (John 21:15-17).

After all that had happened, was Peter still His friend? Yes. Jesus wanted him to be sure of it.

Jesus befriended the disciple Judas Iscariot as well. That friendship did not work out as well as the others. As he embezzled donation money, Judas betrayed his friendship even before he betrayed his Master to the authorities. And yet down to the last moments of His life, Jesus loved Judas as a friend, giving him an opportunity to change his mind. (See John 13:18-30.)

Jesus not only befriended men; He also defied the conventions of the day to befriend women. He reached out to the Samaritan woman at the well, challenging her to give up her sinful lifestyle and drink the living water that would satisfy her every need. (See John 4.) He honored her above even His disciples by revealing first to her that He was indeed the promised Messiah. (See John 4:25-26.)

Jesus was not afraid to identify with the outcasts of society. He offered— and still offers—His friendship to people who do not deserve it. As He put it, *"I have not come to call the righteous, but sinners, to repentance"* (Luke 5:32). Jesus was and is the truest friend a sinner can have (see Matt. 11:19).

## TRUE FRIENDS

The most famous friendship in the Bible is the friendship between two young men, David and Jonathan. David, the former shepherd who had come to King Saul's court after killing Goliath and whose lyre-accompanied psalms had supernatural power over Saul's fits of raging, met Saul's son Jonathan, who was about the same age as David. Their friendship was not a casual one; in fact, soon it became a matter of life and death for David. (These days, conservative Christians tend to disparage close male friendships such as theirs, lest they be considered homosexual in nature.)

YOUR HEART: BONDED WITH OTHERS

In due time, both men were surrounded by armies of loyal soldiers, but at one point when David was defenseless, Jonathan proved his friendship in a unique way. When Jonathan's father Saul discovered that God's hand was upon David to become king in his place, he did everything he could think of to run him off, even to the point of trying to kill him. Jonathan sought David out and helped him to slip away secretly, making excuses for him, providing for his needs, and making sure he was safe. (See First Samuel 18–20 and 23.)

As the years went by, although the two men were grieved by their forced absence from each other, they remained steadfast friends. Years later when Jonathan was killed in battle, David's grief was hard to bear:

> *How the mighty have fallen in the midst of the battle! Jonathan was slain in your high places. I am distressed for you, my brother Jonathan; you have been very pleasant to me; your love to me was wonderful, surpassing the love of women* (2 Samuel 1:25-26).

Later, David made a place at the royal table for Jonathan's crippled son, Mephibosheth, purely out of loyalty to his father's lineage. (See Second Samuel 9.) He didn't have to do that. Most victorious kings would not have done it. But Jonathan had been the truest friend he ever had.

True friends will stick with you. They will come through thick and thin with you. Phony friends will not. Phony friends just talk about being friends. Sometimes, they become more like enemies. (After all, you only have to drop the "r" from *friend* to make it the word *fiend*.)

When Jesus walked the Earth, phony people definitely did not endear themselves to Him, especially those who claimed a false spirituality. In the case of the temple money changers in Jerusalem, His reaction was violent:

> *So they came to Jerusalem. Then Jesus went into the temple and began to drive out those who bought and sold in the temple, and overturned the tables of the money changers and the seats of those who sold doves. And He would not allow anyone to carry wares*

*through the temple. Then He taught, saying to them, "Is it not written, 'My house shall be called a house of prayer for all nations'? But you have made it a 'den of thieves'"* (Mark 11:15-17).

Jesus could not tolerate such travesty in the place that had been built by David's son Solomon a thousand years earlier. From having once hosted the Shekinah glory of God, His Father's house had become a dirty, noisy marketplace where dishonesty ruled. You see, the people could not pay the temple tax with just any kind of money. It had to be paid in temple coinage, which meant that money changers had set up shop to exchange the people's ordinary cash, for a price. Others, with the approval of the priests, had set up concessions where you could purchase "spotless" animals to be used as sacrifices—also at a profit, of course. Every single person in the place, from the priests to the dove-sellers, was a hypocrite. They were doing their deceitful business and performing their ceremonies without knowing or heeding the holy God in whose house they were doing business.

Jesus also expressed how He felt about phonies when He cursed the fruitless fig tree, and He meant it as a lesson for His disciples. The story carries some interesting implications:

*Now the next day, when they had come out from Bethany, He was hungry. And seeing from afar a fig tree having leaves, He went to see if perhaps He would find something on it. When He came to it, He found nothing but leaves, for it was not the season for figs. In response Jesus said to it, "Let no one eat fruit from you ever again." And His disciples heard it* (Mark 11:12-14).

The story mentions that it was not yet the time for figs. Fig season was about five weeks away. Everybody in those days knew what a fig tree looked like. The disciples walking with Jesus knew that fig trees produce their fruit before they are completely leafed out. This particular tree sported luxuriant, green foliage, which was what caught Jesus' eye. Because this tree was already in full leaf long before the other fig trees, Jesus went up to it expecting to find some ready-to-eat figs on it. Such a vibrant specimen of a tree should have produced a great harvest of fruit, more than enough for a hungry man. But His inspection proved the worst—the tree was barren. It only looked good. It promised figs, but failed to deliver on the phony promise.

Woe unto the people of God who are like barren fig trees—long on promises and short on obedient follow-through.

## WHOM CAN YOU TRUST?

How utterly important it is for us to look out for each other as we engage in the spiritual warfare that is entailed in the Christian life! The battles can get ugly. We need allies. And as most of us discover early in life, most friendships will be temporary or seasonal. Only in rare instances will friendships last a lifetime.

The friendships that matter the most are the deepest ones, whether they are lifelong or somehow curtailed by life circumstances. A trustworthy friend will walk the rugged road of life with you, with all its ups and downs. You can trust a true friend with your deepest secrets. A true friend, genuine in his or her own right, accepts you as you are, without trying to modify you. A trustworthy friend is both uncritical and unafraid to intervene when needed, even if it means confronting you with your inconsistencies. A friend who is trustworthy and true will remain available to you at any time or in any place. A choice friend is worth going to war for. You can't find another one easily.

For many people, their very best friend is their spouse. Being married to your best friend is wonderful when you're trying to stand against the powers of darkness. A husband and wife who are not only united in their commitment to marriage and to the Lord, but who are the closest of friends, can make the devil's job very difficult indeed. Being united in marriage and in trust means you are double trouble to the enemy.

In fact, I would go so far as to say that a genuine Christian family is the single most powerful institution on the face of the Earth for opposing the kingdom of darkness. Getting married is an act of spiritual warfare. Getting married declares war on sexual sin and the temptation of lust. Marriage is much more than a marriage license on a piece of paper. It is a spiritual union. Two are much more powerful than one. Two plus God is the strongest of all. *"Though one may be overpowered by another, two can withstand him. And a threefold cord is not quickly broken"* (Eccles. 4:12).

Spiritual agreement means spiritual power. That's why Jesus said, *"Again I say to you that if two of you agree on earth concerning anything that they ask, it will be done for them by My Father in heaven"* (Matt. 18:19). The prophet Amos wrote: *"Can two walk together, unless they are agreed?"* (Amos 3:3).

The corollary to that is that when a married couple or two friends are not in agreement, then power dissipates. The Living Bible puts it this way, *"For how can we walk together with your sins between us?"* (Amos 3:3 TLB).

Naturally, the devil attacks close friendships and marriages with vehemence. He hates them. He introduces unfaithfulness, betrayal, disagreement, violence, and more. He also inspires lawmakers to pass laws that allow watered-down and sinful unions and ungodly behaviors.

These devilish strategies cause havoc, but they do not bring down the Kingdom of God. God's love is stronger still, and He equips the saints with alliances that the enemy cannot replicate. In the words of Martin Luther:

> Though this world, with devils filled
> should threaten to undo us
> we will not fear, for God hath willed
> his truth to triumph through us.[3]

Surrounded by friends who are trustworthy and true, you can fight to the finish with passion.

What kind of a friend are you? On the spiritual battlefield, your welfare and the welfare of others may depend on the bonds and partnerships you have developed over time. In spiritual warfare, the outcome may hinge on the quality of your relationships with other warriors.

Make it your goal to become a true and valued friend, not a fruitless phony.

## ENDNOTES

1. See *Brown, Driver, and Briggs' Hebrew Definitions* (based on *Gesensius' Theological Word Book of the Old Testament*). Hebrew lexicon entry for Ra`ah. The Old Testament Hebrew Lexicon (Strong's number 7462), http://www.searchgodsword.org/lex/heb/view.cgi?number=7462.

2. See *Thayer's Greek Definitions* and *Smith's Bible Dictionary*. Greek lexicon entry for Philos. The New Testament Greek Lexicon (Strong's number 5384), http://www.searchgodsword.org/lex/grk/view.cgi.number=5384.

3. Martin Luther, "A Mighty Fortress Is Our God," c. 1521; words in the public domain.

# Chapter 10

# Your Triumph: Embracing Integrity

*Life Lesson #10: Be a Provider, Not a Pretender*

S omewhere in the hidden recesses of our religious history, we have gotten the idea that being a good Christian means, "Smile a lot and be really nice. Then you will never have to go through really difficult times." If we do face a tough time, we learn to pretend that we're OK. Otherwise, people will accuse us of having a weak faith or falling prey to self-pity.

We have made being a good Christian synonymous with pulling ourselves up by our own bootstraps. We have learned to pretend to be something we are not, and we confuse non-Christians with our inconsistencies. It's as if we wear masks, like the gala throng in that scene from *Phantom of the Opera*. We put on masks that will beautify our sinfulness and help us to attain higher levels of approval and influence.

What specific masks do we most often choose in our dance of pretense?

The *mask of tradition* ensures that we will fit in with the accepted status quo. Wearing it implicitly endorses the importance of institutions over individual men and women; it elevates time-honored doctrines over compassionate responses to human needs. Jesus was not too fond of the way people use their traditions as an excuse for not carrying out obedience to God. He blew apart the mask of traditions as sacred within themselves, and He blasted those who wore such a mask for holding their traditions higher than the oracles of God. "Hypocrites," He called them:

*He replied, "Isaiah was right when he prophesied about you hypocrites; as it is written: "'These people honor Me with their lips, but their hearts are far from Me. They worship Me in vain; their teachings are merely human rules.' You have let go of the commands of God and are holding on to human traditions." And He continued, "You have a fine way of setting aside the commands of God in order to observe your own traditions* (Mark 7:6-9 NIV).

Instead of the mask of tradition (or any other mask), we need to get real. Instead of putting on masks or putting on airs or putting on a show, we should put on the girdle of the truth. We need to put on Jesus Christ Himself: *"...Therefore let us cast off the works of darkness, and let us put on the armor of light....put on the Lord Jesus Christ..."* (Rom. 13:12,14).

The mask of tradition is similar to another mask, the *mask of position*. People in the Church world, just as in the secular world, scramble to acquire positions of power, influence, and status. They assign themselves impressive titles as they groom themselves for success. A prerequisite for wearing this mask includes wealth or the appearance of wealth. A movie-star smile and a handsome family help, too.

Too often, those in high positions of authority do not practice what they preach. This was also true in Jesus' day:

*The teachers of religious law and the Pharisees are the official interpreters of the law of Moses. So practice and obey whatever they tell you, but don't follow their example. For they don't practice what they teach. They crush people with unbearable religious demands and never lift a finger to ease the burden. Everything they do is for show. On their arms they wear extra wide prayer boxes with Scripture verses inside, and they wear robes with extra long tassels. And they love to sit at the head table at banquets and in the seats of honor in the synagogues. They love to receive respectful greetings as they walk in the marketplaces, and to be called "Rabbi" (Matthew 23:2-7 NLT).*

The mask of position drops off in a hurry when the wearer stumbles. Just look at the track record of many leaders, within the Church and outside it, and you will see what I mean. The mask of position provides scanty coverage over the long term.

A third well-known mask is the camouflage of false spirituality. People who wear it want to appear to be spiritual by the standards of those they are trying to impress and even intimidate. They assume "holy" facial expressions and adopt demeanors that match their idea of the holy man or woman of God they want people to think they are. Jesus brushed such impostors off:

> *Woe to you, scribes and Pharisees, hypocrites! For you devour widows' houses, and for a pretense make long prayers. Therefore you will receive greater condemnation* (Matthew 23:14).

## PRETENDERS CANNOT PROVIDE

People who wear such masks can talk a good game, but they never really contribute much. They concentrate on their own welfare at the expense of others. They will tell you, "I'm here for you," but they'll never show up when you're in need. They profess to want to help the church, but when an opportunity arises, they are not the ones toting that barge or lifting that bale. They talk about how they witness for Christ, but they never win a soul to Him. They claim to be sharing in the labor of the ministry, but they find ways to wiggle out of the real work involved.

Do you know somebody like this? Have you worn one of those masks yourself from time to time?

Pretenders have to put all their energy into trying to look good. They cannot provide for the needs of others, especially their families and those who are closest to them. At home is where the mask most often slips off. What does the person really look like? You can tell me, I'm sure, possibly from firsthand experience.

Under the masks, you'll find everything from humdrum personal weaknesses to horrific crimes. Behind the cover-up, you will see:

*...contentions, jealousies, outbursts of wrath, selfish ambitions, backbitings, whisperings, conceits, tumults* (2 Corinthians 12:20).

*...impurity, immorality and sensuality...* (2 Corinthians 12:21 NASB).

*...unrighteousness, fornication, idolatry, adultery, homosexuality, sodomy, thievery, covetousness, alcoholism, reviling, and extortion.* (See First Corinthians 6:9-10.)

*...cowardice, unbelief, corruption, murder, immorality, witchcraft, idol worship, and lying.* (See Revelation 21:8.)

*...wild parties and drunkenness...sexual promiscuity and immoral living...quarreling and jealousy* (Romans 13:13 NLT).

*...immorality, impurity, sensuality, idolatry, sorcery, enmities, strife, jealousy, outbursts of anger, disputes, dissensions, factions, envying, drunkenness, carousing, and things like these* (Galatians 5:19-21 NASB).

That's a lot to try to cover up! All of these things are the opposite of the fruit of the Spirit. At best, they are like cheap, fruit-shaped ornaments hanging on the tree of your life. Needless to say, they don't do anybody any good.

To replace the fake fruit (not to mention the masks) with the real thing, we must allow ourselves to be truly grafted into Jesus. We must allow His pruning to make us healthy and productive. Then, if we continue in Him, our branches will be able to provide abundant fruit for others:

> But I say, walk by the Spirit, and you will not carry out the desire of the flesh....But the fruit of the Spirit is love, joy, peace, patience, kindness, goodness, faithfulness, gentleness, self-control; against such things there is no law. Now those who belong to Christ Jesus have crucified the flesh with its passions and desires. If we live by the Spirit, let us also walk by the Spirit. Let us not become boastful, challenging one another, envying one another (Galatians 5:16, 22-26 NASB).

Those who have crucified the flesh and who walk by the Spirit are the only ones who are true-hearted enough to be spiritual warriors. Sure, you may be able to pass for the real thing. Fooling people isn't all that difficult. But if, in your lifetime, you do not perform Jesus' will by doing His works, it won't matter how many demons you cast out of people.

In contrast to the inconsistency, secretive behavior, and unhealthy independence of a pretender, the fruit of humble, obedient love will make you a true spiritual provider and take you all the way to Heaven:

> So then, you will know them by their fruits. Not everyone who says to Me, "Lord, Lord," will enter the kingdom of heaven, but he who does the will of My Father who is in heaven will enter. Many will say to Me on that day, "Lord, Lord, did we not prophesy in Your name, and in Your name cast out demons, and in Your name perform many miracles?" And then I will declare to them, "I never knew you; depart from Me, you who practice lawlessness" (Matthew 7:20-23 NASB).

# FRUIT OUTSTRIPS SUPERNATURAL ENCOUNTERS

I have to wonder sometimes if people are pulling the "God card" in their attempt to regain standing and status. They claim to have visited the throne room in Heaven, the fires of hell, or both. Some have had legitimate near-death experiences and some (like the apostle Paul himself) may have had "third heaven" experiences (see 2 Cor. 12:2), although it is impossible to objectively prove such claims one way or another.

But I personally have never been to Heaven, and I have never met the apostle Paul. Jesus has never come into my bedroom, sat on the edge of my bed, and had a casual conversation with me. Could it happen to someone? Absolutely. But if it ever happens to you, I'd like to hear about it personally. While you're taking a lie-detector test, I would have you sit down and describe your experience in detail so that I could determine the facts and the circumstances. My point is that we must be very careful of accepting spirituality by pretense and instead objectively test the validity of extra-biblical experiences.

I would also ask you about your history of drug usage, what you've smoked in the past, and what you have been smoking lately...

Why do I seem so dubious? Because so much of this kind of thing can be found in New Age circles as well. While the devil may be only duplicating spiritually authentic experiences, I think that sometimes Christians are trying to duplicate them as well. The human mind has its strange and unplumbed aspects. We can come up with some good tales. When you hear people who are involved in the occult telling the same stories, you know you can't believe every story you hear, even if it comes from the mouth of a fellow Christian. Everyone seems to go through the same tunnel; they see the same white light at the other end. People interpret their experiences through their own philosophical and theological paradigms. Could it be that human beings are wired in such a way as to allow for some universal experiences that happen under stress?

Regardless of where supernatural experiences come from, the worst part ends up being the way they can play into a holier-than-thou way of thinking. I don't want to allow supernatural encounters to become a sign of deep spirituality or holiness or power. I don't intend to use them to validate the truth of the Bible—or my own status in the Kingdom of God. I aim to keep my feet on the ground and my heart in the Word of God, letting psychological/spiritual experiences stay in the realm of speculation and conjecture. They cannot become the basis for my faith, and I do not want others to rely on them either.

At times, such experiences appear to be enemy efforts to divert us from true spiritual warfare. They can delude us into thinking that we never need to slog through the hard work of listening to each other's anguished souls and leading people into inner healing and deliverance. Such experiences can claim to be a quick-fix prescription for spiritual well-being.

## INTEGRITY IN EVERYTHING

People have the idea that spiritual warfare is this exotic thing where mighty, faith-filled, prophetic men and women of God wearing Superman capes are doing all these exploits. In actual fact, the most effective spiritual warfare is being fought by ordinary men and women and children at home, in their families. That is where the values of true faith are instilled and acted out. That's where you take down your mask long enough to see what's underneath. Hopefully, home is where you decide to take God up on His promises to set you free indeed, even if you have to seek outside help to get there.

Your full victory over the devil will never occur unless you embrace integrity in everything. Holiness of life and spiritual power will only become linked in your experience if you accept the hard work of growing to full maturity. Your character should not require a mask in order to look like Him.

As with so many other things, Paul put it best:

*But in all things we commend ourselves as ministers of God: in much patience, in tribulations, in needs, in distresses, in stripes, in imprisonments, in tumults, in labors, in sleeplessness, in fastings; by purity, by knowledge, by longsuffering, by kindness, by the Holy Spirit, by sincere love, by the word of truth, by the power of God, by the armor of righteousness on the right hand and on the left, by honor and dishonor, by evil report and good report; as deceivers, and yet true; as unknown, and yet well known; as dying, and behold we live; as chastened, and yet not killed; as sorrowful, yet always rejoicing; as poor, yet making many rich; as having nothing, and yet possessing all things* (2 Corinthians 6:4-10).

The more "real" you become in Christ and the less often you resort to your old "good Christian" masks, the more effective you will become as a spiritual warrior.

James, the brother of Jesus, wrote,

*But if you have bitter envy and self-seeking in your hearts, do not boast and lie against the truth. This wisdom does not descend from above, but is earthly, sensual, demonic. For where envy and self-seeking exist, confusion and every evil thing are there. But the wisdom that is from above is first pure, then peaceable, gentle, willing to yield, full of mercy and good fruits, without partiality and without hypocrisy. Now the fruit of righteousness is sown in peace by those who make peace* (James 3:14-18).

Ironic as it may seem, you may achieve some of your most ferocious moments on the battlefield in an almost bloodless manner. Your most telling spiritual victories may well occur as you walk in the peace-filled grace of God's Spirit, day in and day out. Paul wrote to the Roman Christians:

*...I want you to be wise in doing right and to stay innocent of any wrong. The God of peace will soon crush Satan under your feet. May the grace of our Lord Jesus be with you* (Romans 16:19-20 NLT).

To crush satan will require transparency. In warring against evil, there is no room for pretense. A provider, one who looks after the needs of his family, his church, and his community, is a true example of a spiritual warrior who does not fall under the condemnation of First Timothy 5:8:

*But if anyone does not provide for his own, and especially for those of his household, he has denied the faith and is worse than an unbeliever.*

# PART II
# ACTIVATIONS

### Ten Prayerful Proclamations
### to Demon-Proof Your Life

This section of the book will help you act on what you have learned. I have paired each of the ten Life Lessons you have just completed with a powerful, focused, declarative prayer. You can use and re-use these statements whenever your circumstances warrant, or, of course, you can build on them using your own words.

Spiritual warfare prayers *demand* results. They don't ask politely. They march into the jaws of hell and tell the devil what the rules are and that he must abide by them. To be aggressive enough to do that, *you* yourself need to know what the rules are, and that's why we have spent so much time talking about them in the first part of this book.

Do not be afraid to talk to the devil, even though you will not have a friendly conversation. He has to shut up and listen to you, because you come in the name and in the authority of the One who took him down, Jesus.

Your active spiritual warfare requires spiritual strategies and spiritual weapons. First I want to sum up practical principles about spiritual warfare prayer. I'll lay out ten preparations for prayer, ten reasons to pray, ten characteristics of spiritual warfare prayer, and ten times to pray spiritual warfare prayers. Then I will give you ten actual statements with which you can declare, proclaim, and establish the victory of Jesus over the specific demonic situations you face in your particular location on the spiritual battleground.

As you take hold of these prayers and proclamations, you will be taking strong offensive action against the enemy—to the point that, as the title indicates, you will be able to make your life genuinely "demon-proof."

## PRAYER IS WAGING WAR

With every breath you take, you engage a world where a battle rages at all times. As you know (though it is easy to forget), that means you need to pray all the time. The Bible says, *"Never stop praying"* (1 Thess. 5:17 NLT). As the forces of darkness wage tumultuous and vindictive war against the forces of the Kingdom of God, each one of us needs to do his or her part.

Every one of us has been born into this battle, and we must participate, whether we want to or not. No one can remain neutral as a malicious devil strives to undermine the loving goodness of God. His forces of darkness attempt to mask the light of God. His wicked counterfeits try to replace the reality of Heaven, and his iniquitous injustice endeavors to trump what's right.

Satan, who is an intelligent strategist and an obstinate fighter, refuses to acknowledge defeat. Our task, as soldiers in the army of God, is to recover lost territory and stolen possessions from the evil one and to defend vulnerable ground in Jesus' name.

As I have made clear throughout the chapters of this book, we fight and stand strong purely because of our position in Christ. We are *"strong in the Lord, and in the power of His might"* (Eph. 6:10). We fight in the strength of God's authority. Our spiritual influence is much greater than we realize most of the time. It can be summed up in these words: *"All authority has been given to Me in heaven and on earth"* (Matt. 28:18), and *"The LORD said to my Lord, 'Sit at My right hand, till I make Your enemies Your footstool'"* (Ps. 110:1), and *"Therefore if you have been raised up with Christ, keep seeking the things above, where Christ is, seated at the right hand of God"* (Col. 3:1 NASB).

God's Word declares:

*Ask Me, and I will make the nations Your inheritance, the ends of the earth your possession. You will break them with a rod of iron; You will dash them to pieces like pottery* (Psalm 2:8-9 NIV).

And He promises:

*He will guard the feet of His saints, but the wicked shall be silent in darkness. "For by strength no man shall prevail. The adversaries of the LORD shall be broken in pieces; from heaven He will thunder against them. The LORD will judge the ends of the earth. He will give strength to His king, and exalt the horn of His anointed"* (1 Samuel 2:9-10).

Your success in waging this war will depend on the level of your obedience to the One who sits on the throne of authority. As a representative of the victorious Christ Jesus, whose Holy Spirit dwells in your heart, you will be able to wield the sword of the Word of God with effectiveness. Evil spirits will flee before you just as they fled before Jesus. They will recognize you as one of His own.

## TEN PREPARATIONS FOR SPIRITUAL WARFARE PRAYER

You may have launched into spiritual warfare prayer, only to discover that you have slammed into an invisible blockade. Don't quit. Take it as an indication that you need to do some further preparatory, prayerful examination of your own life. I have identified ten primary preliminaries that deserve your attention.

### Declare Your Faith

You cannot defeat the devil, get out of your personal misery into freedom, and help others with spiritual warfare prayer until and unless you know Jesus

Christ as Savior and Lord. In other words, if you're going to pray spiritual warfare prayers, first you must make a *declaration of faith*. Having discovered your identity in Jesus Christ, you declare to others that He is their Savior and Lord.

That may sound too simple and basic, but without a declaration of faith, you are still on the devil's side of the equation. You cannot pray a spiritual warfare prayer unless Jesus Christ is your personal Lord and Savior. Unless you're in an ongoing relationship with Him, abiding in Him and allowing His Spirit to abide in you, your prayers and proclamations will be empty words. You can tell the devil to leave you alone all you want to, but he won't go anywhere unless you know Jesus.

Once in a seminar in California, a woman who had seen me on television came to me for help. She had a "ghost" in her house, she told me, and she wanted me to get rid of it. I don't think she realized that the evil entity she was calling a ghost was really a demon, not some dearly departed person whose spirit was wandering in limbo. She didn't like the first question I asked her: "Do you know the Lord Jesus Christ as your own personal Savior?"

She said, "Oh, I just want you to get rid of this ghost. I don't want to talk about all this religious stuff. I don't want to hear about that born-again stuff."

I had to tell her, "Lady, Jesus makes the ghosts go. I don't make the ghosts go. I may be the exorcist, but no ghost or demon is going anywhere because I say so. It's my say-so empowered by the authority of Jesus Christ within me that makes them leave. They won't leave your house until you have the same Jesus in you." That's as far as we got with it. She refused to make any kind of a declaration of faith.

The first preparation for prayer is to make your own confession of faith in Jesus. "Through the blood of Jesus, I am justified by faith. Through His sacrifice on the cross, I have peace." Your authority stems from identifying yourself 100 percent with Him.

## RESIST THE DEVIL

The second preparation for spiritual warfare prayer is to *adopt a stance of resistance*. Resistance implies that you do not intend to give the enemy a chance. You resist him verbally, and you resist him with your lifestyle. You refuse to give the devil any legal reason to attack you. The Bible's exhortation is clear: *"...Resist the devil and he will flee from you"* (James 4:7). You resist the devil every time you resist sin because sin gives the evil one access to your soul. Take seriously the scriptural admonition, *"'Be angry, and do not sin': do not let the sun go down on your wrath, nor give place to the devil"* (Eph. 4:26-27). Give the enemy no place in you. Your anger or other sins can create a place for the enemy to influence you.

Never mind that much of the Church does not resist the devil actively. Too often Christians are afraid of getting imbalanced. Some of them don't want to mention the devil by name because they believe it detracts from honoring Jesus. I do not agree with them. Since Jesus' purpose in coming to Earth was to destroy the works of the devil (see 1 John 3:8), resisting the devil is the name of the game.

## CONFESS YOUR SINS

A third step of preparation for prayer against the devil is simple: *confess your sins.* As I mentioned already, unconfessed sins give the devil a foothold in your life. Confessing your sins to the Lord and repenting of them will leave the devil nowhere to hide in your life.

Ask the Lord to help you see your sins as sin, so that you can confess them. Tell Him you are sorry for them. Be specific. Confess often—morning, noon, and night, if necessary. You are a sinner, and you need the Savior. Confess your sins and allow His blood to cleanse them from you. The people who get slammed by the devil are the ones who don't deal with their stuff, the people who hide things, who are not willing to face the truth about the past. Root out your sins and ask God to repair the damage. Then you can get on with the business of praying effectively against the devil. As I tell people over and over, and as I pointed out earlier, "Get your stuff before your stuff gets you!"

## FORGIVE THE SINS OF OTHERS

Along the same lines, you need to *forgive the sins of others*. That is the fourth step in preparation for praying spiritual warfare prayers. Many of us find it easier to confess our own sins and ask for God's forgiveness than we do to forgive someone else who has hurt us. And yet the Word tells us:

> *If you bring your gift to the altar, and there remember that your brother has something against you, leave your gift there before the altar, and go your way. First be reconciled to your brother, and then come and offer your gift* (Matthew 5:23-24).

"*Something against you*" can include unforgiveness or bitterness in your heart toward somebody who has offended you—a fractured relationship, a bad business deal, an immoral sexual situation, an emotional or spiritual violation of your integrity. Whatever may have happened, the Bible message is sobering:

> *Then his master...said to him, "You wicked servant! I forgave you all that debt because you begged me. Should you not also have had compassion on your fellow servant, just as I had pity on you?" And his master was angry, and delivered him to the torturers until he should pay all that was due to him. So My heavenly Father also will do to you if each of you, from his heart, does not forgive his brother his trespasses"* (Matthew 18:32-35).

You must forgive other people if you're going to pray aggressive and effective prayers of spiritual warfare. If you lack a forgiving heart, the devil will exploit that fact. You can't just put a Band-Aid on hurtful situations. You need to really go back and forgive the other person and get cleansed. This may require some time of inner healing. But if you don't do this work, your prayers won't work.

Your forgiveness doesn't even have to be emotionally complete. Sometimes the wounds are still fresh. Here is a prayer I often have people pray: "Lord, I know that I need to forgive. I don't feel like forgiving, but I acknowledge it's the way of the cross. It's what You did to Your tormentors. So, Lord, I speak forgiveness by faith, and I await the confirmation of my feelings that Your Holy Spirit has allowed me to emotionally grasp the forgiveness in my heart."

## BREAK UNGODLY SOUL TIES

Fifth, you need to *break ungodly soul ties*, and you need spiritual warfare prayers to do it. Your soul is the real "you," your individuated identity, the seat of your thoughts, emotions, and decisions. When you tie your soul in an ungodly way to another person, you compromise your freedom. Many people carry soul ties with old boyfriends or old girlfriends, ex-spouses, abusive former pastors, and sometimes with satanic priests or fake prophets. It might have been a professional relationship. You may have been part of a church where you lived under constant intimidation from the pastor. Even if you leave the situation, your soul can remain bound to the pressure or to the bad doctrine that the pastor has come to represent.

If you have become enmeshed with any person, walking with him or her in unity of purpose and decisions, you are no longer free to stand up in the freedom of an exclusive bond with Jesus. The tie can consist of sexual, emotional, or spiritual bonds. You came together with someone, and your souls mingled and meshed. Unintentionally, you situated the bond in your soul with that person higher than your bond with your Lord.

The healthy soul tie we are to engage is an intimate relationship with Jesus. In several places, Paul described this as a servant-master relationship (see Rom. 1:1; 1 Cor. 9:19; 2 Tim. 2:24). You can't get much closer than that, to be bound as a bond-servant to absolute obedience and fidelity as a slave is to his master. The Bible also describes this heavenly soul tie in spousal terms, Christ as the groom and believers as His bride (see Rev. 19:7; 21:2).

When you have negatively bound yourself to another person, although it may have been in the distant past, you will no longer be able to operate out of wholeness. Your spiritual warfare prayers will be hindered. The Bible makes it very clear:

> *Do not be unequally yoked together with unbelievers. For what fellowship has righteousness with lawlessness? And what communion has light with darkness? And what accord has Christ with Belial? Or what part has a believer with an unbeliever?* (2 Corinthians 6:14-15).

You can break soul ties by praying declaratively: "I break the soul tie with _____, in the name of the Lord Jesus Christ."

## RELEASE YOURSELF FROM INHERITED BONDAGE

In addition to breaking soul ties, you must consider how to *release yourself from inherited bondage.* You cannot pray effective spiritual warfare prayers until you have broken generational curses and until you have cleansed the evil out of your bloodline. Again, you need to pray spiritual warfare prayers for your own freedom in order to go on to pray successful spiritual warfare prayers on behalf of others.

You must leave no stone unturned; often you will need the help of others to discern what has been buried in the past, lost to living memory, but still working its damage in your life to this day. Each of us has many ancestors, and all of them were sinners. With the help of the Holy Spirit, identify all vows, oaths, blood covenants, ceremonies, sorceries, witchcraft, false gods, and so forth, and break each bondage in the name of Jesus.

The roots of your physical, mental, emotional, and spiritual heritage go back to before you were born. Besides breaking off the bonds, you will need a combination of inner healing and, often, deliverance. You will be glad you made the effort when you see your prayers getting answered as never before.

## BREAK OCCULT CURSES

If you or your family members have been involved with occult practices in the past, you have contracted relationships with the kingdom of darkness. Those agreements with darkness will not go away until you make them go away. They will not fade with the passage of time or disappear simply because you no longer engage in the occult practices. You can't assume immunity from harmful effects from even one-time actions such as reading your horoscope, having tarot cards read, or consulting a psychic or a fortune-teller.

Any occult activities, regardless of how fleeting, can hinder your prayer. You may not notice any significant hindrance to your daily life, but when you start to pray prayers of spiritual warfare, you may come up short and wonder what's wrong.

*Break occult curses and spells*, release yourself and your property from bewitchment, command charms to become powerless, and decree that jinxes should not continue to operate. Pray, "Lord, if any of these things—[make a list]—are hindering my prayers in any way, I break their hold over me and put them under Jesus' shed blood."

### Take Authority Over the Strongman

Jesus said,

> *Every kingdom divided against itself is brought to desolation, and every city or house divided against itself will not stand. If Satan casts out Satan, he is divided against himself. How then will his kingdom stand? And if I cast out demons by Beelzebub, by whom*

*do your sons cast them out? Therefore they shall be your judges.*
*But if I cast out demons by the Spirit of God, surely the kingdom*
*of God has come upon you. Or how can one enter a strong man's*
*house and plunder his goods, unless he first binds the strong man?*
*And then he will plunder his house* (Matthew 12:25-29).

A kingdom will be divided against itself when two serious authorities contend for dominance. In order to wage war against the "strong man," the devil or one of his more powerful subordinates, you need to *take authority over the strongman* in a concerted way. Then you can plunder the house of evil that he has built.

Satan makes it his business to build a literal architecture of evil in human lives, an infrastructure that can serve his purposes. He doesn't simply walk in a door you left open and relax in a recliner with a beer. No, he starts looking around at every possible piece of your life that he can get his fingers on. He begins to build, and he adds on to the structure continually until you have a massive web of destruction inside you.

The only way you can dismantle this superstructure is to deal with the strongman who's behind it. Who is in charge of the operation? It's as if you wanted to dismantle the Ford Motor Company. Would you visit a local assembly line and confront a worker who was putting bolts on car doors, or would you go straight to the top, to the chief executive? Obviously, you would go straight to the strongest authority in the company.

In the same way, you need to locate and go after the strongman who has engineered the unwelcome superstructure inside you. You may have to wear down some of his minions first, but eventually you need to go after the one who is calling the shots. Once you have weakened and dismantled the work of the evil one inside, your spiritual warfare praying will be unbound and powerful.

## COMMAND SATAN TO RELEASE WHAT HE HAS STOLEN

Think about spiritual and temporal resources that once belonged to you. Figure out what to call them: "health," "family unity," "marital happiness," "peace," "joy," *et cetera*… What happened?

You need to *command satan to release what he has stolen* from you and from others. Get aggressive. For everything the enemy has stolen from you, you can say, "Yes, I want it back now, sevenfold, in the name of Jesus."

The Bible principle is that when a thief gets captured, he must repay sevenfold what he has stolen. *"If he [a thief] is caught, he must pay sevenfold, though it costs him all the wealth of his house"* (Prov. 6:31 NIV). Don't settle for less.

## CLAIM BACK LOST GROUND

Claiming back what the devil has stolen from you is similar to the tenth preparation for spiritual warfare prayer: *claim back lost ground.*

The only way to get it back is through spiritual warfare praying. Satan is a thief and a robber. He came into your life without invitation, and he took territory from you—health, money, friends, family, and more. He may have conquered territory from your ancestors, and you may have suffered as a result. Claim it back, with interest.

## TEN REASONS TO PRAY SPIRITUAL WARFARE PRAYERS

I can think of at least ten good reasons to pray spiritual warfare prayers. Every follower of Jesus prays for the same basic reasons.

### 1. Pray to prepare.

Pray to get ready to fight. It's too late to start praying when the enemy has a gun to your brain. Begin to pray before the bullet is in the chamber. Pray to put on the armor of God. You need to put it on *before* you step onto the battlefield. Jesus prayed in preparation for His death. Before He went to the cross, He prayed His heart out in the Garden of Gethsemane. His prayers won Him the supreme grace He needed in order to endure the abuse and go through with the torture of death by crucifixion.

### 2. Pray to drive out the devil.

When the disciples failed to cast out some demons, Jesus told them, *"This kind does not go out except by prayer and fasting"* (Matt. 17:21). Sometimes, in other words, the devil will only obey commands that have been reinforced with prayer ahead of time. Remember also the power of agreement when two or more people pray for the same thing. (See Matthew 18:19-20.)

Some people get hung up on the *fasting* word. They assume that if they go without eating, they can get rid of demons as if it's some kind of a guarantee. They don't understand the purpose of fasting. Fasting is supposed to change your mindset, to focus your attention, to get your spirit in the right place for spiritual warfare. It's not about the lack of food; it's about you being ready to fight.

### 3. Pray to take action.

Joshua blew the trumpet, but he also took up the sword. (See Joshua 5 and 6.) Prayer and spiritual warfare empowers the work, but the battle may also entail going out into the trenches and engaging in hand-to-hand combat. You pray to take possession of the promises, but you have to get out and take the land. You have to pray and fast to get the job done, often. The devil won't give up just because you use Jesus' name or because you got born again. He's not going to flee because you prayed the sinner's prayer back in 1979, and he's not going to leave you alone because you are busy serving in your church. You have to pray yourself into action.

### 4. Pray to have passion.

You have to have passion, and the only way to get enough passion is to pray for it. You have to pray as if you really mean it. The devil won't take you seriously if you pray passive, pathetic, whiny prayers. ("Pretty please, God, help me do this. If it be Your will....") You don't have to wonder if it's God's will to, for example, protect your children from harm. Go ahead and get worked up about it: "Satan, keep your hands off my kids! Get out! Now!"

### 5. Pray to be committed.

Act as if it's a matter of life and death—because it *is*. Importunity is essential. Pray that you can keep warring against the lies and injustices of the enemy without flagging, like the importunate widow in the Bible. (See Luke 18:1-7.) About that widow's persistent praying, Jesus said:

> *Hear what the unjust judge said. And shall God not avenge His own elect who cry out day and night to Him, though He bears long with them?* (Luke 18:6-7).

### 6. Pray to resist ungodly opposition.

Intercede to scatter the agents of evil who may come against you physically or spiritually. Command their opposition to be broken up and neutralized, not out of personal antagonism, but out of godly determination to succeed in your divine assignments. Yes, the Bible tells us to turn the other cheek and to go the second mile, but there's a time *not* to do it, too. When the devil's trying to do a number on you and he's using some human being to do it, you're not supposed to roll over like a circus lion. You won't have to become nasty or difficult. Just resist the devil. Keep him out of your family and out of your life.

### 7. Pray to invalidate evil reports.

Come against evil accusations that have been brought against you illegitimately by the kingdom of darkness. Cancel them, in the name of Jesus. Satan, the accuser, planted them. Root them up as soon as you become aware of them in the conduct of people around you.

> *No weapon formed against you shall prosper, and every tongue which rises against you in judgment you shall condemn. This is the heritage of the servants of the* Lord, *and their righteousness is from Me," says the* Lord (Isaiah 54:17).

### 8. Pray against spells and curses.

Defy every operation of darkness that has been commissioned against you. Insist that every mission of the evil one be aborted, in the name of Jesus. Send evil maledictions back where they came from. You're not looking for revenge. You're just standing up as one of God's anointed priests—and every one of us is a priest in the Kingdom—striking down every evil word that comes against you, reminding the devil that it can be dangerous to attack God's anointed ones. *"But you are a chosen generation, a royal priesthood, a holy nation, His own special people, that you may proclaim the praises of Him who called you out of darkness into His marvelous light"* (1 Pet. 2:9).

### 9. Pray against every evil arrow.

The forces of darkness are assembled against the forces of the Kingdom of light, and they fire their arrows at God's people day and night. Pray against the withering rain of fiery arrows that otherwise will deplete and dishearten you. Take hold of your faith, which is your shield. Get it up! Hold high *"the shield of faith with which you will be able to quench all the fiery darts of the wicked one"* (Eph. 6:16).

10. Pray against every evil presence in your own being.

Do self-deliverance. Seriously—it's a good idea. Command that all oppression break off you and that attacks of sickness and disease be blocked. In the beginning, you may need somebody to help you out, because you won't be able to see the forest for the trees. You may need someone to get the process going for you. But after a while, you will need to stand strong on a daily basis, in the power of the Spirit of God. Other people can't do this for you. You will need to muster your spiritual resources in order to fight. Get rid of the junk that keeps coming onto you from the devil. You can pray, "God, if there is anything in me that is not supposed to be there, I want it out right now." Command it to leave. The devil may walk into your bedroom in the midnight hour. You are the only one who can tell him to leave. Learn how to pray the kinds of prayers that drive him nuts, so he'll start leaving you alone.

Become a disturber of the peace—the devil's false sense of peace, that is. More than once, as I have ministered to someone, demons have made this remark: "You are disturbing things! Everything was fine without you." I come along, and I introduce conflict. I make demands. I give commands. I speak out in Jesus' name, and evil spirits cannot tolerate that. They thought they had it made in the shade until I brought the spotlight of God to shine on their wicked designs.

Spiritual warfare will seem to stir up trouble at first. It will make you dig where you have never dug before. It will cause you to keep looking and probing until every last vestige of what the devil has done in your life has been rooted out in the name of Jesus.

Then you will find that you are well on your way to being conformed to the image of Christ. He is unsullied by evil and unperturbed by the actions of the dark spirits who oppose Him. You, too, can be like that, increasingly. Stay as close to Jesus as the breath is close to your lungs. Your peace consists of the presence of your Lord, Jesus, and that peace prevails over every conflict you will ever face.

## TEN CHARACTERISTICS OF
## SPIRITUAL WARFARE PRAYERS

As you can see from everything I have been telling you, your spiritual warfare prayers cannot be considered true spiritual warfare prayers unless they are:

1. *Unapologetic*—prayed without the slightest regret, never entertaining a single thought of whether or not the request should have been uttered.

2. *Insistent*—dogged and persistent, unshakable in the pursuit of the answer.

3. *Bold*—intrepid and fearless, having the brazen courage to demand a response.

4. *Unwavering*—steadfast, unswerving eyes fixed on one goal: the elimination of the enemy.

5. *Aggressive*—hard-hitting and bold in every petition.

6. *Demanding*—imperative, pressing for an immediate response.

7. *Expectant*—filled with positive anticipation of victory.

8. *Militant*—combative and assertive, fighting like a front-line soldier.

9. *Urgent*—compelling, crying out to God for immediate intervention.

10. *Persevering*—tenacious and untiring, pushing past every discouragement or doubt about the outcome.

Each one of these ten characteristics portrays a variation on the theme of spiritual combat. You will never get answers to your spiritual warfare prayers unless you press the devil to the ground with them. You must be absolutely steadfast, with no wiggle in your words and no relaxation in your efforts.

The persistent widow in Jesus' story gives us a good picture of the kind of prayers that get results. That little woman was undeterred by the impossibilities of her situation. To get justice from her adversary, the evil judge had to stop sitting on her case. No way was she going to put up with inaction or delay. She wanted justice *now*, and she let her voice be heard until she got it. Read the story in a contemporary translation to refresh its message:

> One day Jesus told His disciples a story to show that they should always pray and never give up. "There was a judge in a certain city," He said, "who neither feared God nor cared about people. A widow of that city came to him repeatedly, saying, 'Give me justice in this dispute with my enemy.' The judge ignored her for a while, but finally he said to himself, 'I don't fear God or care about people, but this woman is driving me crazy. I'm going to see that she gets justice, because she is wearing me out with her constant requests!'" (Luke 18:1-5 NLT)

Be persistent and be *insistent*. Don't be timid. Don't be afraid to raise your voice. There's something about the very way you utter spiritual warfare prayers that makes a difference. I have heard some beautiful prayers intoned in rich baritone voices by prestigious men of the cloth. I'm not sure God bothered to listen to them, and I'm quite sure that the devil laughed at them. God was not impressed, and the enemy was not distressed. Those men were basically talking to themselves and making every effort to impress their congregations. What's the point of praying if the prayers miss the mark?

You need to pray with aggression because you are in a fight. Satan will not back down because you whispered, weeping, "Please...if it be God's will." He has no compassion whatsoever. He knows only the language of warfare. This means that most of your prayers should be loud, although not always. Whether loud or not, spiritual warfare prayers exert pressure on the enemy. They never, never, never give up.

Patience is not an attribute of a spiritual warrior. Perseverance is, but patience implies acquiescence to a situation. Your prayers *demand*; they do not request. Your prayers demand action *now*, not later on today or sometime tomorrow.

Some Christians seem to think that eventually the devil will get tired of hearing Jesus' name, and he'll go away. I don't know where they get that idea. Satan will not go anywhere until he's told to go, in no uncertain terms. He never leaves a place until he gets kicked out.

Militant prayers are imperative. They are not suggestions. They sound combative. They get in the devil's face. They come up against him. They challenge. They insist, unapologetically, that something needs to change immediately. Spiritual warfare prayers sound urgent, because the need is pressing. You can't wait until tomorrow. Tomorrow may be too late.

Spiritual warfare prayers are tenacious, and spiritual pray-ers have a reputation for hanging on unrelentingly. They know that *unbelief* and its resulting passivity are their worst challenges. They know that *doubt* kills faith. They build themselves up in their faith, and they surround themselves with fellow warriors who will reinforce their belief in the saving, restorative power of Jesus Christ: *"But you, dear friends, must build each other up in your most holy faith,* [and] *pray in the power of the Holy Spirit"* (Jude 20:20 NLT).

Breathlessly, we await the desired result. As if we're jumping up and down with eagerness inside, we hold onto our expectant faith. "It's coming! It's almost here! It's going to happen soon!" With that attitude, spiritual warfare prayers never go unanswered.

## TEN TIMES TO PRAY
## SPIRITUAL WARFARE PRAYERS

Don't limit your definition of "spiritual warfare." If you think spiritual warfare consists mostly of prayers for deliverance uttered by a seasoned exorcist either in the context of corporate worship or on a televised hotline, you will miss 99 percent of the action. All Christians, you as well as me, should be praying spiritual warfare prayers all the time. Everywhere you go, you should be on the lookout for opportunities.

I can think of ten types of situations that demand spiritual warfare prayers. You will find yourself in all of them at various points in your life.

### 1. When loved ones are lost.

When family members and friends walk apart from God, you must contend for their salvation. Well-directed spiritual warfare prayers will find their mark regardless of how hopeless the situation may seem. Jesus said:

> *Those who are well have no need of a physician, but those who are sick. I did not come to call the righteous, but sinners, to repentance* (Mark 2:17).

Before sinners can be born again, somebody must pray to heal their spiritual blindness and deafness, so that they:

> *…no longer walk as the rest of the Gentiles walk, in the futility of their mind, having their understanding darkened, being alienated from the life of God, because of the ignorance that is in them, because of the blindness of their heart* (Ephesians 4:17-18).

Somebody needs to love them enough to fight the darkness on their behalf. That somebody may be you.

## 2. When your family needs protection.

Your prayers may be all that stand in the way of harmful assaults of the enemy. As you know, the devil roams around like a hungry lion (see 1 Pet. 5:8). He sets his sights on anybody who appears to be vulnerable. When you have raised up spiritual protection on behalf of your loved ones, your prayers and faith-declarations stop the enemy in his tracks. You defeat him before he gets started. Satan complained to the Lord God that Job (before his trials began) was untouchable:

> *So Satan answered the Lord and said, "Does Job fear God for nothing? Have You not made a hedge around him, around his household, and around all that he has on every side? You have blessed the work of his hands, and his possessions have increased in the land"* (Job 1:9-10).

Satan wanted to bring Job to ruin, but as long as God's hedge of protection remained, he could not do anything to him.

## 3. When your children need to know they are safe.

Part of the role of a soldier is reassurance for the ones he is protecting and defending. They need to know that somebody is looking out for them. As you stand firm on the spiritual battlefield on behalf of your children, tell them what you are doing. Expose them to your faith. Make conversation about God a normal part of your family life. Teach your children how to trust God themselves. Demonstrate how faith in God is like a strong guardrail to keep His faithful ones on the track, out of trouble, and safe.

## 4. When you are under spiritual attack.

This one is obvious enough. When you find yourself under pressure, bowing under the weight of condemnation, confusion, negative thoughts, discouragement, depression, or any kind of oppression, take action! You need help from God, and the only way to get it is to pray. God will rescue you.

*He will also keep you firm to the end, so that you will be blameless on the day of our Lord Jesus Christ. God is faithful, who has called you into fellowship with His Son, Jesus Christ our Lord* (1 Corinthians 1:8-9 NIV).

### 5. When you need to deal with besetting sins.

Too often, spiritual attacks take the form of temptation to sin, and your habitual, familiar sins will seem the most tempting to you. In your own strength, resisting such temptations will seem impossible. You don't even *want* to resist them.

*Each one is tempted when he is drawn away by his own desires and enticed. Then, when desire has conceived, it gives birth to sin; and sin, when it is full-grown, brings forth death* (James 1:14-15).

Pray spiritual warfare prayers to get God's help. Cry out to Him. He will hear and respond.

### 6. When you are afflicted by sickness and disease.

Jesus is the Great Physician, able to heal any ailment, major or minor. To judge by His responses to people in the Bible accounts, He likes to have people demand His healing attention. The blind beggar Bartimaeus cried out so loudly that the other bystanders tried to hush him. What did he do then? He cried out even more loudly. And Jesus healed him. (See Mark 10:46-52.) A Gentile mother was unreasonably insistent:

*...a woman of Canaan came from that region and cried out to Him, saying, "Have mercy on me, O Lord, Son of David! My daughter is severely demon-possessed"* (Matthew 15:22).

Jesus resisted her at first, but then, impressed by her persistence:

*Jesus answered and said to her, "O woman, great is your faith! Let it be to you as you desire." And her daughter was healed from that very hour* (Matthew 15:28).

### 7. When your finances are faltering.

When you need money and the provisions that money can supply, you can use the words of the mighty warrior-king, David, who prayed for protection for himself and his people and for prosperity:

*Blessed be the LORD my Rock, who trains my hands for war, and my fingers for battle—...Rescue me and deliver me from the hand of foreigners, whose mouth speaks lying words, and whose right hand is a right hand of falsehood—...That our barns may be full, supplying all kinds of produce; that our sheep may bring forth thousands and ten thousands in our fields; that our oxen may be well laden; that there be no breaking in or going out; that there be no outcry in our streets* (Psalm 144:1,11, 13-14).

*O my God, I trust in You; let me not be ashamed; let not my enemies triumph over me....Who is the man that fears the LORD? Him shall He teach in the way He chooses. He himself shall dwell in prosperity, and his descendants shall inherit the earth* (Psalm 25:2,12-13).

In the spirit of David's psalms, the apostle John knew that prayer was the only way to approach practical needs: *"Beloved, I pray that you may prosper in all things and be in health, just as your soul prospers"* (3 John 2:2).

### 8. When you are facing momentous decisions.

Do not make life-changing decisions without the protection and guidance of God's Spirit. Take Moses' words as your own: *"Then he [Moses] said to Him, 'If Your Presence does not go with us, do not bring us up from here'"* (Exod. 33:15).

You know that once you make your decision, you are going to need to keep relying on God to complete the task at hand: *"Unless the LORD builds the house, they labor in vain who build it; unless the LORD guards the city, the watchman stays awake in vain"* (Ps. 127:1).

### 9. When you are not certain of God's will for your life.

How many times do we say, "If it be Thy will, Lord"? If you really do want to know the will of God, you will have to seek it out. You will have to pursue it. Ask confidently:

> *If any of you lacks wisdom, let him ask of God, who gives to all liberally and without reproach, and it will be given to him. But let him ask in faith, with no doubting, for he who doubts is like a wave of the sea driven and tossed by the wind* (James 1:5-6).

Pray for doors to open—and to close. With God, a door is a door of guidance, whether He permits you to enter through it or prevents you from making a mistake by doing so. You belong to Him now, and you want His will, not your own, to direct your life. In all likelihood, you won't be able to step onto the path of God's will until you pray as Jesus did: *"...not My will, but Yours, be done"* (Luke 22:42).

10. When you are ministering to someone bound by the devil.

To be an effective spiritual warrior when you are ministering to someone else, you do not need a college degree in deliverance techniques. All you need is the Spirit of Jesus telling you what to do next and an awareness of the three avenues through which the enemy has gained control over the person before you. Although the devil comes at us with many different tricks, he can find only three ways to worm his way into a person: (1) *"the lust of the flesh,"* (2) *"the lust of the eyes,"* and (3) *"the pride of life"* (1 John 2:16).

The lust of the flesh consists of the human desires that are contrary to the will of God. Our fleshly bodies belong to the created world. Upon our deaths, our bodies will return to the dust of the earth from whence they came; they cannot enter the Kingdom of God. Naturally, the world system influences them, pitting the desires of our bodies against the desires of the Creator. The devil is cognizant of this fact, so he uses human flesh as his stronghold.

In order to lust after something with your flesh, you must first see the thing—thus, the *"lust of the eyes."* The devil plants attractions before your physical eyes as well as in your mind's eye. He realizes that you may start to desire whatever he can cause you to fix your eyes upon. He tempts you.

When David glimpsed Bathsheba on the rooftop, he began to lust after her. (See Second Samuel 11.) The lust of his eyes became the lust of his flesh. The lust of his flesh, together with his kingly pride, persuaded him that he should take her as his own.

The pride of life is never far removed from the lusts of our eyes and bodies. Pride is the devil's province. Pride caused lucifer to be cast out of Heaven. The proverb is true: *"Pride goes before destruction, and a haughty spirit before a fall"* (Prov. 16:18).

As I have detailed throughout this book, the devil can only infiltrate a person's life through openings created by sinful actions. Ministry to other people always involves spiritual warfare because human nature is the primary battlefield on which the kingdom of darkness clashes with the Kingdom of God's light.

## JOYFUL, OBEDIENT PRAYER

Your future as a spiritual warrior is in your own hands. Take your calling seriously, yet with profound joy. The happiest people are always the ones who are the freest inside their spirits and souls. Like the apostle Paul, make it your goal to step free of the devil's entanglements and to stay free:

> ...*You are now ashamed of the things you used to do, things that end in eternal doom. But now you are free from the power of sin and have become slaves of God. Now you do those things that lead to holiness and result in eternal life* (Romans 6:21-22 NLT).

You are striving for a heavenly crown. Paul tells you to run the race like a well-trained soldier:

> *Do you not know that those who run in a race all run, but one receives the prize? Run in such a way that you may obtain it. And everyone who competes for the prize is temperate in all things. Now they do it to obtain a perishable crown, but we for an imperishable crown. Therefore I run thus: not with uncertainty. Thus I fight: not as one who beats the air. But I discipline my body and bring it into subjection, lest, when I have preached to others, I myself should become disqualified* (1 Corinthians 9:24-27).

Make it a race that the "great cloud of witnesses" (see Heb. 12:1) will appreciate seeing—bring as many others with you as you can. Paul wrote to the Christians in Rome, "*Now I am going to Jerusalem to minister to the saints*" (Rom. 15:25). May you set your face like flint and go to your "Jerusalem," which could be anyplace in the world, to minister to your fellow believers and to bring unbelievers to faith.

A tormented world needs you, now. Jesus sends you, saying, *"Behold, I send you out as lambs among wolves"* (Luke 10:3). Have you heard His call? Are you ready and willing? The rewards of obedience lie straight ahead.

I'm on my feet now, ready to go. Are you? Get those warfare prayers ready. Let's roll!

# Activation 1

# Your Destiny: Seizing the Reason You Are Here: Declaration of a Spiritual Warrior

*Before I formed you in the womb I knew you, before you were born I set you apart...* (Jeremiah 1:5 NIV).

Before the worlds were formed my destiny was determined by God.

In my mother's womb, before my first breath, God released my destiny.

The Holy Spirit has been guiding me all my life toward my destiny.

It is God's will that I discover my destiny, and I receive it now.

If demons have bound my destiny in any manner, in Jesus' name,

I renounce every legal right that deters my destiny!

I pull down every stronghold that binds up my destiny!

I break every curse that diverts my destiny!

I submit my entire being to Jesus Christ who holds my destiny in His hands.

No power in Heaven, on Earth, or in hell can take it from Him.

He purchased my destiny at the cross with His blood.

The strongman who holds back any part of my destiny must release it, now!

Satan, I command you in the name of Jesus:

Loose my calling to serve God with all my heart!

Release my anointing to walk in wisdom and understanding!

Unleash my purpose to heal the brokenhearted and set the captives free!

I will achieve my destiny.

I will overcome by the blood of the Lamb.

I will become the person I was always meant to be.

I will walk in the blessing and favor that God has promised me.

I will not turn back nor turn aside.

No power of people or demons will keep me from my destiny.

Until I am with my Lord eternally, my destiny shall be my constant compulsion.

My destiny awaits me, and I await my destiny.

© Bob Larson 2011

# Activation 2

# Your Calling: Standing Firm Like David: Oath of a Spiritual Warrior

*But the LORD is with me like a mighty warrior...*
(Jeremiah 20:11 NIV).

I AM A WARRIOR!

Jesus Christ is my Commanding Officer.

The Bible is my code of conduct.

The Word of God is my weapon of warfare.

I AM A WARRIOR!

I volunteered to serve and enlisted for eternity.

I will not get out or sell out.

I am faithful and reliable.

I AM A WARRIOR!

I do not need to be pampered.

No one has to encourage me.

I salute my King and obey His orders.

I AM A WARRIOR!

I do not need to be coddled.

I am committed without reservation.

Demons can't defeat me, and critics can't discourage me.

I AM A WARRIOR!

Disappointment will not turn me aside.

A loss will not make me to quit.

I am more than a conqueror through Christ.

I AM A WARRIOR!

Money can't buy me, and hell can't stop me.

Death can't destroy me. I will not give up.

I march into battle under the banner of Christ.

I AM A WARRIOR!

© Bob Larson 2011

Activation 3

# Your Identity: Turning Obstacles Into Opportunities: Pledge of a Spiritual Warrior

*The God of peace will soon crush Satan under your feet...*
(Romans 16:20 NIV).

I AM A WARRIOR!

My foe is satan.

I won't be bullied by his threats or fooled by his distractions.

I see his evil all around me, but I will not retreat from battle.

I pledge to fight, with victory as the only option.

I AM A WARRIOR!

My battle isn't for an hour or a day.

I know the struggle will be relentless as long as I live.

I am committed to keeping my eye upon the enemy.

I pledge to wield my sword until my last breath.

I AM A WARRIOR!

I'm not fighting for a truce or treaty.

I don't need rest to escape the battle.

I'll accept nothing less than total defeat of satan.

I pledge to wage war until the work of the devil is destroyed.

I AM A WARRIOR!

I am winning all day every day.

I can't lose because my Lord has already won.

I won't heed the call to quit and lay down my weapons.

I pledge with my very life to defend what God has given me.

I AM A WARRIOR!

I sing the song of praise and jubilation.

I shout the cry of triumph over evil.

I am persuaded that nothing can keep me from God's love.

I pledge to sing the victor's song no matter how goes the battle.

I AM A WARRIOR!

© 2011 Bob Larson

Activation 4

# Your Character: Do You Have What It Takes? Affirmation of a Spiritual Warrior

*For if the trumpet makes an uncertain sound, who will prepare for battle?*
(1 Corinthians 14:8)

I am a warrior because my salvation demands that I serve.

I have no choice but to show bravery in battle.

I fight not for vainglory or for temporary victories.

I am a warrior for reasons that affect time and eternity.

I am a warrior because I have been drafted into God's army.

I serve proudly as a soldier fighting for the cause of His Kingdom.

I fight because there is no other choice worthy of my Savior.

I am a warrior who will fight until I take my last breath.

I am a warrior because the lies of satan must be confronted.

I won't give in to the deceptions of one who murders and lies.

I stand up for what's right, and I declare God's Word.

<hr style="opacity:0.15" />

I am a warrior defending truth in the face of error that is all around me.

I am a warrior, and the accusations of satan do not deter me.

I refuse to listen to his lies about my motives or my choices.

I know my heart, and that I have no condemnation in Christ.

I am confident that my Commander will not forsake me.

I am a warrior fighting with courage, determination, and faithfulness.

I desire the mind of Christ and every emotion has been surrendered to Him;

I surrender my feelings to the higher call of God in Christ.

I am a warrior marching in step with God's will for my life.

I AM A WARRIOR!

© 2011 Bob Larson

# Your Strength: Weakness Transformed: Armor of a Spiritual Warrior

*Put on the whole armor of God, that you may be able to stand against the wiles of the devil* (Ephesians 6:11).

I am a soldier in the Lord's army.

I am ready to wage spiritual warfare.

I am prepared to fight against the forces of darkness.

I will not be deterred by defeat.

I stand and put on the armor of God.

I begin with the BELT OF TRUTH.

It holds all my other armor in place.

It is engraved with these words: "Jesus Christ is the way, the truth, and the life!"

I protect myself with the BREASTPLATE OF RIGHTEOUSNESS.

This armor protects my vital, spiritual organs.

It guards my heart, my mind, and my emotions.

With this breastplate, I become the righteousness of God in Christ.

I place the GOSPEL OF PEACE on my feet.

These shoes help me stand firmly in my faith.

On life's journey I will walk in the right direction.

The peace of God, which passes understanding, will guide my steps.

I take up the SHIELD OF FAITH.

No matter what satan hurls my way I will be protected.

This shield will stop every fiery dart of the devil.

With faith I can please God and utterly defeat the enemy.

I put on the HELMET OF SALVATION.

This headgear will deflect doubt and discouragement.

It reminds me that I am saved and on my way to Heaven.

This helmet will keep me safe in my salvation.

In my hand I grasp the SWORD OF THE SPIRIT.

The Word of God is my offensive weapon.

I wield the Word with confidence and authority.

"Thus saith the Lord" will be my battle cry in spiritual combat.

I am now prepared: clad in God's armor.

So let the battle begin—I declare war on the devil and all his demons.

There is no place for retreat, and I am ready to live and die for my Lord.

I am a soldier in the Lord's army.

© 2011 Bob Larson

Activation 6

# Your Voice: Making a Positive Difference: Reliability of a Spiritual Warrior

*Preach the word! Be ready in season and out of season. Convince, rebuke, exhort, with all longsuffering and teaching.* (2 Timothy 4:2)

I have been called by God to teach by example and actions.

I am steadfast to fulfill that calling.

Understanding that all of life is a spiritual combat zone,

I will stand strong against the enemy of my soul.

I will demonstrate God's power in every aspect of life.

I can be depended upon to stand and fight evil.

Knowing that I can conquer through Christ,

I will speak the truth whatever the consequences.

Others may preach what a Christian should do.

I will do what Jesus did and show faith in action.

Caring not what others may think or say,

I will put on God's armor and use it to win against satan.

I know that the battle for my soul may be long and arduous.

I will be dependable and not shrink from conflict.

Hearing the call of the Word to stand and be strong,

I will resist the devil in whatever way he attacks my life.

I will teach by showing others perseverance in my walk with Christ.

I am steadfast in my convictions and firm in my faith.

Believing that with God all things are possible,

I will not fear any obstacle that evil spirits put in my way.

I will not merely preach what is right, but demonstrate it.

I will keep learning and growing in spiritual wisdom.

Being aware that satan uses ignorance as one of his devices,

I will study God's Word to know how to fight with the sword of Spirit.

© 2011 Bob Larson

# Your Strategy: Outgiving the Enemy: Generosity of a Spiritual Warrior

*Give, and it will be given to you: good measure, pressed down, shaken together, and running over...* (Luke 6:38).

I choose to give as Christ gave that I might have a life full of joy.

I will give back even as I have received.

I choose to be a giver, not a taker.

I choose to give in abundance that I may receive in abundance.

I will be motivated by sacrifice, not selfishness.

I could hold back part of it, like Ananias and Sapphira in the Bible,

But instead I choose to give what I have, liberally and cheerfully.

As a warrior, I give so the windows of Heaven's blessings may be opened.

I could focus on what I might lose by giving,

But I choose to concentrate on what I will gain by giving.

I could be the kind of person always wanting more,

But I choose to be God-centered, not me-centered.

I determine to give who I am, not just what I have.

Instead of wishing I had given less,

I will think of how I could have given more.

By sowing good seed, I will reap a good harvest.

I choose to give back to God what was His before He loaned it to me.

I will release my offerings to the Lord when I give.

I could complain about how my gifts are being used,

But I choose to give with proper motives and leave the rest to Him.

As a strategy in the spiritual battle, I choose to be a cheerful giver.

I will offer the Lord not only my financial resources,

But I will also give Him my very self.

In total surrender to Jesus, I give my person and my pocketbook.

© 2011 Bob Larson

# Your Exploits: Goals Straight Ahead: Goals of a Spiritual Warrior

*For exaltation comes neither from the east nor from the west nor from the south. But God is the Judge: He puts down one, and exalts another* (**Psalm 75:6-7**).

I declare that I will not live in a world of fantasy and imagination.

I reject big dreams that accomplish little.

Instead, my life will have a solid foundation that is durable and lasting.

I will have reasonable expectations that don't overreach.

I will not be like those who constantly scheme in the abstract,

Who seldom do anything concrete that is measurable.

I will build on past successes, one at a time,

So that I can reach the goals that the Holy Spirit has put in my heart.

I will not promise more than I can produce,

So that God may get the glory because of His strength at work through me.

I will not be like those who overestimate their capabilities,

Who blame others when they falter or fail on the spiritual battlefield.

I will faithfully labor with the gifts and talents God gave me,

So that God can bless my faithfulness and open the doors He wants to open.

I will not be like gamblers waiting for the next roll of the dice,

Who always look for the next big win.

I will work hard and be faithful in all that I do, no matter how humble,

So that my accomplishments may truly be promotions from the Lord.

My dreams will not be inflated with wishful thinking.

I refuse to go from one overstated idea to the next.

I see those who dream, but never achieve lasting results.

They focus on avoiding pain instead of achieving gain.

As for me, I embrace my calling and anointing from the Lord.

My goal is to hinder the forces of evil and to destroy the works of the enemy.

© 2011 Bob Larson

# Your Heart: Bonded With Others: Dependability of a Spiritual Warrior

*A man who has friends must himself be friendly...* (Proverbs 18:24).

I have the choice of being a friend or a phony.

A true friend is dependable and trustworthy.

In an age of fleeting values and shallow relationships,

I will be a spiritual warrior whom others can count on.

I will be known as someone who keeps secrets, not one who tells them,

A reliable companion who is there when others need me.

In the war for souls that wages all around me,

I will be a solid soldier watching the back of fellow Christians.

I will offer others unconditional acceptance rather than critical judgment.

I believe that a close relationship requires communication free of criticism.

When the forces of evil try to divide the Body of Christ,

I will stand and fight the accuser of my brothers and sisters in Jesus.

I will be available anytime for a friend in need; I will never be too busy.

A comrade in spiritual arms leaves no one behind.

When satan attacks followers of Christ,

I will be there for them on time and without hesitation.

I will make friends not only with those whom I like, but also with those I dislike.

Jesus Christ commands me to follow His example.

Knowing how Jesus loved Peter even after his betrayal,

I can learn to be the friend of those who have wronged and ill-treated me.

I will enlarge the circle of people I help; I will not restrict it.

I know that a dependable Christian serves as many as possible.

While the world says, "Be careful to help only those who help you,"

I will be as the Good Samaritan who befriended a man he didn't know.

© 2011 Bob Larson

Activation 10

# Your Triumph: Embracing Integrity: Integrity of a Spiritual Warrior

*But if anyone does not provide for his own, and especially for those of his household, he has denied the faith and is worse than an unbeliever*
(1 Timothy 5:8).

As a spiritual warrior, I must be known by my loyalty.

God help me to do what I say I will do.

I will not be a pretender who makes bold promises I never intend to keep,

But rather a provider who has integrity to be true to my word.

As a soldier for the Lord, my word must be kept at any cost.

God help me to not pledge to do what I cannot do.

I will not be a pretender who makes bold statements without counting the cost,

But rather a provider who is reasonable in what I promise to do.

As I oppose the attacks of the enemy, I will be truthful.

God help me to not make hasty vows I can't perform.

Rather than a pretender who wears a mask of hypocrisy to hide my true intentions,

I will be a provider who is transparent in every word and deed.

As a servant of God, my reliability will be beyond question.

God help me to be on the front lines even in the heat of spiritual battle.

Keep me from being a pretender who tries to be something I am not,

But rather a provider who meets my obligations on time and in full.

As a spiritual combatant, I will be honest in all things.

God help me say what I mean and mean what I say.

Keep me from honoring You with my lips while my heart is far from You.

I refuse to hide my intentions or my motives.

As a warrior for God's Kingdom, I must be like my Commanding Officer.

God help me to embrace spiritual honor in all I do and say.

Keep me from being a pretender who loves power and position,

And allow me to be a provider with a servant's heart and a humble attitude.

© 2011 Bob Larson

# BOB LARSON
## AUTHOR, PASTOR, RADIO & TV HOST
*The world's foremost expert on cults, the occult, and supernatural phenomena.*

---

## PERSONAL TIME WITH BOB LARSON

Are you depressed?  Lack direction in life?
Struggle with relationships?  Suffer financial lack or ill health?

## LEARN THE KEYS TO SPIRITUAL SUCCESS!

To arrange for your personal, one-on-one SPIRITUAL ENCOUNTER
with Pastor Bob, email Bob@boblarson.org or call 303-980-1511.

---

Bob Larson's resources are available online. Let Bob's DVD's, books, and
specials help you in your journey to spiritual freedom!

www.boblarson.org
www.demontest.com
www.therealexorcist.com
www.centerforspiritualfreedom.com

Follow Bob Larson's insights and action items
on his blog page @ www.boblarson.org

# IN THE RIGHT HANDS, THIS BOOK WILL CHANGE LIVES!

Most of the people who need this message will not be looking for this book. To change their lives, you need to put a copy of this book in their hands.

> *But others (seeds) fell into good ground, and brought forth fruit, some a hundred-fold, some sixty-fold, some thirty-fold* (Matthew 13:8).

Our ministry is constantly seeking methods to find the good ground, the people who need this anointed message to change their lives. Will you help us reach these people?

> *Remember this—a farmer who plants only a few seeds will get a small crop. But the one who plants generously will get a generous crop* (2 Corinthians 9:6).

## EXTEND THIS MINISTRY BY SOWING
### 3 BOOKS, 5 BOOKS, 10 BOOKS, OR MORE TODAY,
#### AND BECOME A LIFE CHANGER!

Thank you,

Don Nori Sr., Founder
Destiny Image
Since 1982

# DESTINY IMAGE PUBLISHERS, INC.

*"Speaking to the Purposes of God for This Generation
and for the Generations to Come."*

## VISIT OUR NEW SITE HOME AT
## WWW.DESTINYIMAGE.COM

## FREE SUBSCRIPTION TO DI NEWSLETTER

Receive free unpublished articles by top DI authors, exclusive
discounts, and free downloads from our best and newest books.
**Visit www.destinyimage.com to subscribe.**

Write to:    Destiny Image
             P.O. Box 310
             Shippensburg, PA 17257-0310

Call:     1-800-722-6774

Email:    orders@destinyimage.com

For a complete list of our titles or to place an order
online, visit www.destinyimage.com.

FIND US ON FACEBOOK OR FOLLOW US ON TWITTER.

www.facebook.com/destinyimage     facebook
www.twitter.com/destinyimage      twitter